RHEILFFORDD ERYRI

traveller's guide

WELSH HIGHLAND RAILWAY

Published by the Festiniog Railway Company

Harbour Station, Porthmadog, Gwynedd, LL49 9NF

Telephone: 01766 516024

www.festrail.co.uk

Written by Tony Russell

ISBN: 978-0-901848-27-7

Front Cover Photo: **Michael Baker**

Produced by Snowdonia Design & Print, Porthmadog LL49 9NZ

Croeso

Bydd 2022 a 2023, yn nodi 100 mlynedd ers sefydlu Rheilffordd Eryri. Mae hanes digon amrywiol i'r rheilffordd gyda chyfnodau hir pan oedd y rheilffordd ar gau yn gyfan gwbl. Ond rydyn ni'n falch iawn o'r hyn sydd bellach yn un o brif atyniadau Gogledd Cymru. Mae'n ymestyn rhyw 25 milltir o fwrdeistref Frenhinol hanesyddol Caernarfon, ar hyd llethrau'r Wyddfa ac o'r naill arfordir i'r llall, ac ymlaen i dref harbwr Porthmadog.

Efallai fod y pandemig diweddar wedi newid y ffordd rydyn ni defnyddio'r rheilffordd bellach, ond mae yna dda ym mhob drwg. Mae rhanwyr Perspex wedi'u gosod ar lawer o'n cerbydau, sy'n galluogi'r teithiwr a'i gyfeillion i gael eu gofod eu hunain, a gwneud y daith ychydig yn fwy personol. Gallwch hyd yn oed fanteisio ar un o'n hamperi picnic blasus sydd wedi dod yn fwyfwy poblogaidd.

Wrth i'r rheilffordd ymlwybro trwy gefn gwlad anghysbell a gorsafoedd bychain, treuliwch funud neu ddau yn ystyried yr holl ymdrech sydd wedi mynd i wneud eich taith yn bosibl. Mae miliynau o bunnoedd o gyllid cyhoeddus a chyllid preifat, ynghyd â miloedd o ddyddiau o lafur gwirfoddol a llawer iawn o frwdfrydedd wedi cyfuno i wireddu'r freuddwyd hon. Mae'r locomotifau stêm wedi'u hadfer yn hyfryd ac yn gweithio'n galed wrth iddyn nhw ddringo i fyny'r copa, ac mae cerbydau sydd wedi'u hadeiladu gan ein crefftwyr ein hunain yn coroni'r cwbl.

I'ch cynorthwyo i gael y gorau o'ch taith, cafodd y teithlyfr hwn ei lunio i roi gwybod i chi mewn ffordd hawdd a chyflym beth sydd i'w weld drwy ffenestr eich cerbyd. Mae gan bob rhan o'r daith ei thudalennau ei hunan, ynghyd â map gyda nodiadau, lluniau a gwybodaeth ysgrifenedig ynghylch yr hyn y gallwch ei weld o'ch cwmpas. Does ond angen troi at yr adran berthnasol pan fyddwch yn camu ar y trên a dilyn y daith o'r fan honno.

Gallwch weld bwrlwm byd natur a golygfeydd godidog trwy'r ffenestr, yn cynnwys mynyddoedd ac afonydd, gweilch a dyfrgwn. Ceir hanes a chwedlau gyda'r hen adeilad sydd wedi'i adfer yn gariadus yng Nghyffordd Tryfan, a chwedl wych Gelert, y ci a roddodd ei enw i Feddgelert. Mae llefydd i chi grwydro, ar feic neu ar droed efallai. Gyda chymaint i'w wneud yn yr ardal, beth am ddod yn ôl rywbryd eto?

Mae Rheilffordd Ffestiniog ac Eryri yn falch o fod yn rhan o Safle Treftadaeth y Byd Tirwedd Llechi Cymru Unesco, ac mae gwybodaeth ar gael yn y canllaw hwn sy'n adrodd hanes ei chysylltiadau a'r diwydiant llechi.

A phan gyrhaeddwch adref? Cadwch y llyfr hwn wrth law a bydd y lluniau'n eich atgoffa o harddwch Parc Cenedlaethol Eryri a'r rhan arbennig iawn hon o Gymru. Gobeithio eich bod wedi mwynhau eich ymweliad, ac edrychwn ymlaen at eich gweld chi eto!

Paul Lewin
Rheolwr Cyffredinol.

Clare Britton
Rheolwr Masnachol.

Welcome

Croeso Cynnes – A Warm Welcome to the Welsh Highland Railway.

2022 and 2023 see the 100th anniversary of the Welsh Highland Railway, a chequered history with many years of controversy and closure. But we are justly proud of what is now one of North Wales' premier attractions; stretching from the historic Royal Borough of Caernarfon, coast to coast across the foothills of Snowdon, and on to the harbour town of Porthmadog, a distance of some 25 miles.

The recent pandemic may have reshaped the way we use the railway now, but not all change is bad. Many of our carriages have been fitted with Perspex dividers giving the traveller and their companions their own space, making it a little more personal. You can even take on board one of our tasty picnic hampers which have become increasingly popular.

As the line twists and turns through remote countryside and tiny stations, please spare a moment to reflect on just how much has gone into making your journey possible. Millions of pounds of public and private funding, together with thousands of days of volunteer labour and a huge amount of passion have combined to make this dream come true. The beautifully restored steam locomotives working hard as they climb up to the summit, and carriages built by our own craftsmen, complete the picture.

To help you get the most from your journey, this Traveller's Guide has been designed to provide a quick and easy reference to what is outside your carriage window. Each section of the route has its own pages, complete with an annotated map, photographs and written information on what to see around you. Simply turn to the section where you board the train and follow the journey from there.

Nature is in abundance with mountains and rivers, ospreys and otters and some fantastic vistas laid out before you. There is history and legend with the old building at Tryfan Junction Halt lovingly restored and the wonderful tale of Gelert, the dog that gave Beddgelert its name. There are places to explore, perhaps by bike or on foot. With so much to do in the area, why not come back another day?

The Ffestiniog & Welsh Highland Railways are proud to be a part of the Unesco Wales Slate World Heritage Site and there is information throughout this guidebook which tells the story of its slate connections.

And when you get home? Leave this book on the table and the photographs will remind you afterwards of the beauty of the Snowdonia National Park and this very special part of Wales. We hope you have enjoyed your visit and look forward to seeing you again!

Paul Lewin
General Manager.

Clare Britton
Commercial Manager.

A Brief History of the Welsh Highland Railway

Above: *Welsh Highland Railway C1930s*
Below: *Standard-gauge meets narrow-gauge at Dinas Junction in the 1930s*

Unlike the Ffestiniog Railway, the Welsh Highland Railway was not built as one complete line connecting mountain slate quarries to ships berthed at coastal ports.

The Ffestiniog Railway was constructed between 1833 and 1836 deliberately to link the slate quarries around Blaenau Ffestiniog with the harbour at Porthmadog.

However, the Welsh Highland Railway you are enjoying today follows routes that opened between the 1820s and 1920s. Charles Spooner of the Ffestiniog Railway proposed a new narrow gauge line linking the standard gauge London and North Western Railway at Dinas Junction with Rhyd Ddu at the foot of Snowdon in 1872. It was built between 1877 and 1881 and was originally called the North Wales Narrow Gauge Railways. It was used to transport both passengers and dressed slate nine and a half miles (15kms) from the Glanrafon Slate Quarry near Rhyd Ddu to Dinas Junction (see page 16). Spooner also instigated the construction of a three-mile (4.8kms) narrow-gauge branch-line from Dinas to the quarries above Bryngwyn (see pages 46-47).

WELSH HIGHLAND RAILWAY
PRIVILEGE TICKET
Issued in exchange for P.T. order at one fourth ordinary single fare and subject to conditions on the back hereof.

DINAS
TO
PORTMADOC

Third Class   Fare 8d.

Above: *Beddgelert Station in the early 1920s*
Left: *Pen-y-Mount Junction between the Welsh Highland Railway and the Welsh Highland Heritage Railway*
Below: *"Russell" at Beddgelert Station in the early 1920s*

It wasn't until 1923 that the Dinas to Rhyd Ddu line was extended south from Rhyd Ddu to link up with the Croesor Tramway, which had been built in 1864 to connect slate quarries in the Croesor valley with Porthmadog. The completed line, now called for the first time the Welsh Highland Railway, came into service on 1st June 1923. However, it was never a financial success, the anticipated slate and mineral traffic never materialised and even the passenger service was only viable during the summer months when tourists visited Snowdonia in sufficient numbers. The railway was placed in receivership in 1927 and then leased to the Ffestiniog Railway in 1934, but this did nothing to stem the losses and the WHR was closed to passengers at the end of the holiday season in 1936 and finally closed to goods traffic the following year. In 1941, during World War II both the track and rolling stock were requisitioned by the Ministry of Defence.

Over the next twenty years the disused track bed gradually deteriorated, then in 1961 the Welsh Highland Railway Society was established, later becoming the Welsh Highland Railway (1964) Co. Ltd. This was based at Gelert's Farm, Porthmadog, where they opened a stretch of line on the adjacent Beddgelert siding. This line is still in operation today and known as the Welsh Highland Heritage Railway.

In 1989 the Ffestiniog Railway decided to renew its interest in the WHR and made a bid for the original track bed. In 1995, following several years of legal entanglement and a public enquiry (with intervention by the then Secretary of State for Transport John Prescott) the Ffestiniog Railway gained control of the Welsh Highland Railway from the Official Receiver. In the same year the Millennium Commission awarded a grant of £4.3 million to the Ffestiniog Railway towards the re-construction of the WHR between Caernarfon and Rhyd Ddu. It was time to bring the Welsh Highland Railway back to life! (see pages 40-41)

A Journey from Porthmadog to Caernarfon

1 Harbour Station Porthmadog

There has been a railway station at the western end of the sea wall known as The Cob since 1836. It was originally built as the terminus for slate being transported from the quarries in the mountains around Ffestiniog to ships berthed at the nearby harbour. The station opened to passengers on 6th January 1865 and continued to offer a passenger service until the outbreak of the Second World War, closing on 15th September 1939. During the war the station buildings were used as the headquarters and billet of Dutch commandos. A memorial plaque in Spooner's café commemorates this fact. The station re-opened to passengers on 23rd July 1955 and has been in operation ever since.

In 2011 Harbour Station also became the departure point for the newly restored Welsh Highland Railway and in March 2014 a £1.1 million project was completed which allowed trains from both the Ffestiniog and the Welsh Highland Railways to be at station platforms at the same time.

As the name suggests, this station is situated adjacent to Porthmadog Harbour, which has a long and fascinating history. Just a couple of minutes' stroll will bring you to the centre of the harbour and its Maritime Museum, which is housed in one of the original slate storage sheds (see pages 39 of this guidebook for further information).

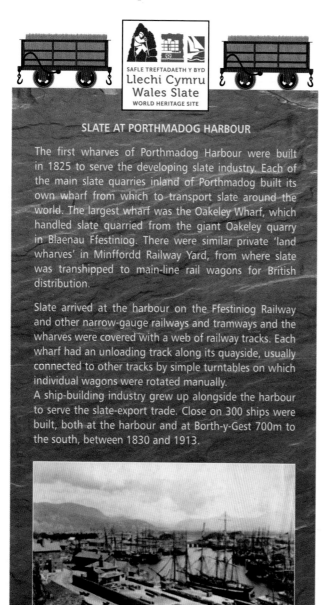

SAFLE TREFTADAETH Y BYD
Llechi Cymru
Wales Slate
WORLD HERITAGE SITE

SLATE AT PORTHMADOG HARBOUR

The first wharves of Porthmadog Harbour were built in 1825 to serve the developing slate industry. Each of the main slate quarries inland of Porthmadog built its own wharf from which to transport slate around the world. The largest wharf was the Oakeley Wharf, which handled slate quarried from the giant Oakeley quarry in Blaenau Ffestiniog. There were similar private 'land wharves' in Minffordd Railway Yard, from where slate was transhipped to main-line rail wagons for British distribution.

Slate arrived at the harbour on the Ffestiniog Railway and other narrow-gauge railways and tramways and the wharves were covered with a web of railway tracks. Each wharf had an unloading track along its quayside, usually connected to other tracks by simple turntables on which individual wagons were rotated manually.

A ship-building industry grew up alongside the harbour to serve the slate-export trade. Close on 300 ships were built, both at the harbour and at Borth-y-Gest 700m to the south, between 1830 and 1913.

2 Porthmadog Harbour

Just outside Harbour Station the track of the Welsh Highland Railway crosses Britannia Bridge (originally constructed in 1810) and the main Porthmadog high street (A487) – always a point of excitement. As it does, there are splendid views to the south-west across Porthmadog Harbour, which owes its existence to the nearby sea wall known as The Cob. The construction of the sea wall in 1811 diverted the course of the River Glaslyn, squeezing it through sluice gates at the western end of the embankment. At the release point beyond the gates, such was the water's power that it scoured out a deep-water channel which was subsequently developed into the Harbour. Originally surrounded by a series of wharves used to transfer slate onto ships waiting at dock, today the Harbour is a haven for leisure boats and where the Victorian slate storage warehouses once stood, modern-day housing and holiday accommodation have now been built.

Top: *Porthmadog Harbour*
Below: *Welsh Highland Railway crossing Britannia Bridge*

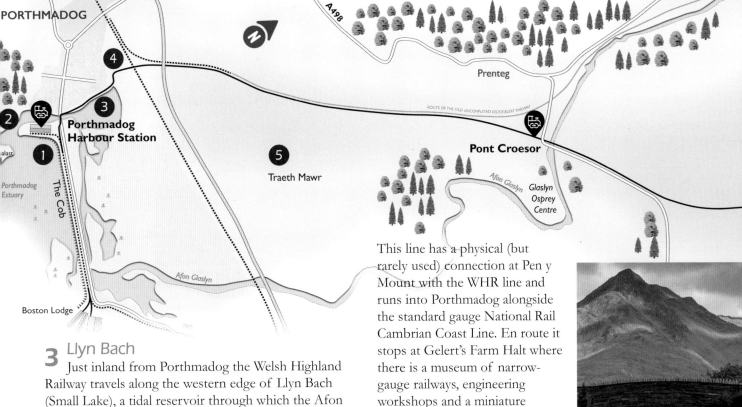

Prenteg

ROUTE OF THE OLD UNCOMPLETED BEDDGELERT RAILWAY

Porthmadog
Harbour Station

Pont Croesor

Traeth Mawr

Afon Glaslyn

Glaslyn
Osprey
Centre

Porthmadog
Estuary

The Cob

Afon Glaslyn

Boston Lodge

3 Llyn Bach

Just inland from Porthmadog the Welsh Highland Railway travels along the western edge of Llyn Bach (Small Lake), a tidal reservoir through which the Afon Glaslyn River flows on its way to the sea. Llyn Bach was originally created in the early years of the 19th century as part of a flood control system for nearby Porthmadog and its Harbour. It is especially popular with birdwatchers and an ideal place to watch waders such as oystercatcher, lapwing and curlew, as well as cormorants, egrets, herons and just occasionally during the summer months ospreys from the nest further upstream.

4 Cae Pawb and Pen y Mount Junction

Cae Pawb is where the Welsh Highland Railway crosses over the standard-gauge Network Rail Cambrian Coast Line, which runs all the way from Pwllheli to Birmingham, via the west Wales coast. You will know when the crossing is made as the train will momentarily clatter.

Near Pen y Mount, you may observe a short length of narrow-gauge track running alongside the Welsh Highland Railway line you are travelling upon. This is a section of the original Welsh Highland Railway track (which was operational from 1922 until 1936) that has been restored by a group of railway enthusiasts volunteering for the Welsh Highland Heritage Railway.

This line has a physical (but rarely used) connection at Pen y Mount with the WHR line and runs into Porthmadog alongside the standard gauge National Rail Cambrian Coast Line. En route it stops at Gelert's Farm Halt where there is a museum of narrow-gauge railways, engineering workshops and a miniature railway, which visitors to the Welsh Highland Heritage Railway site can enjoy.

5 Reclaimed Land of Traeth Mawr

Between Pen y Mount and Pont Croesor the line crosses the flatlands of Traeth Mawr (Big Estuary). Up until the construction of The Cob sea wall at Porthmadog in 1811, the land on either side of the train would have been underwater and the cliffs visible to the north-west would have marked the boundary of the sea as it swept inland towards the hills and mountains around Nantmor and Aberglaslyn.

Dating back to the Ordovician Period some 400 million years ago, these cliffs are made of dolerite, a dark igneous rock that was formed from the volcanic activity that was prevalent in the region at that time. The rock is quite 'blocky' and relatively easy to grip, which is why a section of cliff, located to the east of Tremadog at Bwlch y Moch (otherwise known as the 'Tremadog Slabs') has become a popular climbing and training ground for rock climbers and mountaineers.

Above: *Ancient and Modern as heritage train snakes between the two new tubular bridges that serve as farm crossings*

Left: *Crossing the Network Rail Cambrian Coast Line.* (John Ellis Williams)

7

Left: *Cnicht and the Moelwyns.*
(Tony Russell)

Below: *Bywyd Gwyllt Glaslyn Osprey Visitor Centre from Pont Croesor Station*
(Tony Russell)

6 Pont Croesor

As part of the restoration of the Welsh Highland Railway, the station at Pont Croesor was officially re-opened on 26th May 2010. It takes its name from the adjacent bridge, Pont Croesor, which is one of three railway crossing points over the Afon Glaslyn River. It is also the point where the train crosses the B4410 road which links the villages of Garreg Llanfrothen on one side of Traeth Mawr with Prenteg on the other. Prior to the land being reclaimed from the sea at the beginning of the 19th century, the only way to cross the estuary at this point was by ferry.

At this station you will notice a 200 metre-long track 'loop' with a platform on either side of the two lines. This allows up and down trains to pass each other on this otherwise single-track railway. The train normally waits here for a few minutes while the crew exchange the 'single line token', a safety feature that ensures there is only ever one train on the same section of single-track at any one time.

There are two visitor attractions close to Pont Croesor Station. The centre for the Bywyd Gwyllt Glaslyn Osprey Project is located on the banks of The Afon Glaslyn River and can be seen from the train as it crosses the Pont Croesor Bridge. Plas Brondanw the ancestral home and garden of Portmeirion architect Sir Clough Williams Ellis is situated in the village of Garreg Llanfrothen a mile to the east of Pont Croesor Station.

7 Cnicht and the Moelwyns

Between Pont Croesor and Nantmor there are fine views of the mountains both to the west and the east of the line. Rising to the west are Moel Ddu (Black Bare Hill) 1814 feet (553m) and Moel Hebog (Bare Hill of the Hawk) 2569 feet (783m), both great walks with excellent views to the western coast of Wales. To the east is the magnificent panoramic vista of the Moelwyns. Running from right to left they are Moelwyn Bach (Small) 2329 feet (710m), Moelwyn Mawr (Big) 2530 feet (770m) and Cnicht (known today as 'The Little Matterhorn' because of its pyramidal shape) 2260 feet (689m). The actual name 'Cnicht' is said to derive from the old English

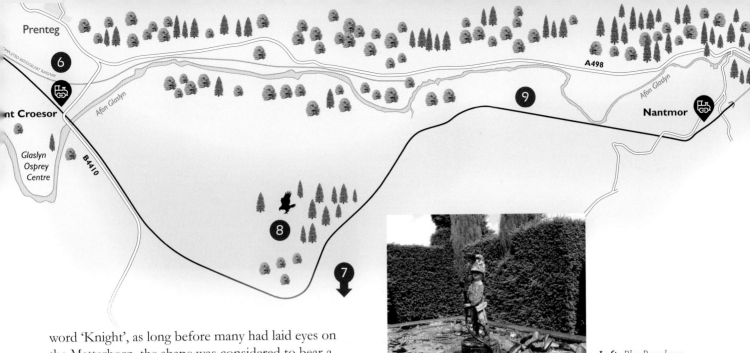

word 'Knight', as long before many had laid eyes on the Matterhorn, the shape was considered to bear a similarity to a knight's helmet.

8 Glaslyn Ospreys

It is without doubt the Moelwyns that command attention on this stretch of the journey, but if you look out of the opposite windows of the train, you may spy a green camouflage caravan, tucked in amongst the trees. This is one of the protection hides for the Glaslyn ospreys that nest each summer in the top of a silver fir tree just a few hundred yards from this spot. It is possible to see the nest from the train and if you ask, the guards may point it out to you as the train passes. These are breeding ospreys and so throughout the season a dedicated band of volunteers keep 24-hour watch on the nest, to ensure the adults and their chicks are not disturbed in any way (see page 53).

9 Hafod y Llyn

Just south of Nantmor is Hafod y Llyn, which translates from Welsh as 'the summer farm building near the lake'. There is an old stone barn close by which the name is believed to refer to and the lake is in the woods on the western side of the line. For a while during the restoration and rebuilding of the Welsh Highland Railway line Hafod y Llyn was the southern terminus. The station opened to passenger traffic on 21st May 2009, but then closed a year later when the next section of line to Pont Croesor opened and station services became operational there.

Occasionally, during the winter months, a limited return service runs from Porthmadog Harbour Station to Hafod y Llyn (there is no passenger alighting at this point). Terminating trains here avoids the steep gradients of the line onward to Beddgelert, thereby allowing lighter locomotives to be used whilst larger locomotives are undergoing their winter maintenance. There is a loop in the line here, which allows the engines to 'run round' from one end of the train to the other.

Left: *Plas Brondanw Gardens* (Tony Russell)

Below: *The line of the old Croesor Tramway near the village of Croesor* (Tony Russell)

SAFLE TREFTADAETH Y BYD
**Llechi Cymru
Wales Slate**
WORLD HERITAGE SITE

THE CROESOR TRAMWAY

For part of your Welsh Highland Railway journey between Pont Croesor and Beddgelert, you are travelling along the route of the old Croesor Tramway.

The Croesor Tramway was a 2 foot (610mm) narrow gauge railway line built in 1864 to carry slate from the Croesor slate quarries which were located between the mountains of Cnicht and Moelwyn Mawr (both clearly visible to the east of the train) to ships berthed at Porthmadog.

Slate quarrying in Cwm Croesor expanded rapidly in the 1860s, but transportation from this remote region to the shipping wharfs at Porthmadog quickly became a limiting factor. Before the tramway was built, the slate used to be hauled by mules over the ridge at the head of the valley and down to the Ffestiniog Railway line at Tanygrisiau, a long and dangerous route. The construction of the Tramway helped enormously, and it continued to carry slate from the quarries right up until its closure in 1944. Having lain derelict for almost 60 years, the section from just north of Pont Croesor to Porthmadog was rebuilt as part of this Welsh Highland Railway route and reopened on 8th January 2011.

10 Nantmor

Before the sea wall at Porthmadog (known as The Cob) was completed in 1811, the village of Nantmor marked the tidal highpoint of the Glaslyn Estuary and sea-going boats were able to navigate their way towards the village and berth in a pool immediately to the south side of Pont Aberglaslyn Bridge, the foundations of which are believed to date back to the 17th century. Nantmor is much older than the current bridge and is documented as being the home of renowned Welsh bard Dafydd Nanmor (died C. 1490) who took his name from the hamlet.

Nantmor and its surroundings were used as the location for the 1957 film, *The Inn of Sixth Happiness* starring Ingrid Bergman and based on the true story of Gladys Aylward a British missionary working in China just before the Second World War. During filming, a representation of part of the Great Wall of China was built in the mountains above Nantmor!

Immediately to the north of Nantmor Station the Welsh Highland Railway travels through three tunnels built between 1906 and 1923. The longest is 280 metres (919 feet) and until the Railway closed the tunnels in the autumn of 2000, in preparation for rebuilding the railway, it was a popular route for walkers.

Top Left: *Nantmor Station*
Top Right: *Entering the tunnels in the Abergalslyn Pass*
Above: *Walkers on the Fisherman's Path below the line of the Welsh Highland Railway*

11 Aberglaslyn Pass

Just south of Beddgelert, be sure to have your cameras ready, as the Welsh Highland Railway enters perhaps the most scenic part of its journey – the Aberglaslyn Pass. Once voted by National Trust members as their favourite site in Britain, this spectacular mountain gorge, through which the fast-flowing Afon Glaslyn river descends from its source high on Snowdon to the sea at Porthmadog, has been an inspiration for poets and artists since the 18th century. One of the most famous artists to have painted here was J.M.W. Turner, who produced several works of the Bridge and Pass during his visit in 1799. Today, Aberglaslyn is one of the most popular tourist destinations within the Snowdonia National Park and still attracts many artists and poets, as well as kayakers, photographers and anglers, who are undoubtedly inspired by the salmon which still leap up these majestic falls in the autumn.

Running immediately below the train is the Fisherman's Path, a rocky trail linking Beddgelert with Nantmor that follows the riverbank and enables visitors to walk right through the Pass. At the Beddgelert end of the Aberglaslyn Pass the train curves across the iron-girder Bryn-y Felin bridge and this is a good place for passengers on-board, as well as walkers to catch a glimpse of the locomotive as it majestically crosses the river.

12 Beddgelert

Beddgelert Station is one of the main stopping-off points for passengers travelling on the Welsh Highland Railway. The village (see our Beddgelert feature on pages 18 & 19) has long been a popular destination for walkers and from Beddgelert Station there are well-marked footpaths leading south towards Nantmor and north towards Rhyd Ddu.

For those continuing their journey on the Welsh Highland Railway, it is a good place to alight from the train for a few moments to admire the locomotives whilst they take on water. With its two platforms and section of double track, Beddgelert Station is also one of the places where trains travelling from the opposite directions of Caernarfon and Porthmadog on this single-track railway can pass each other.

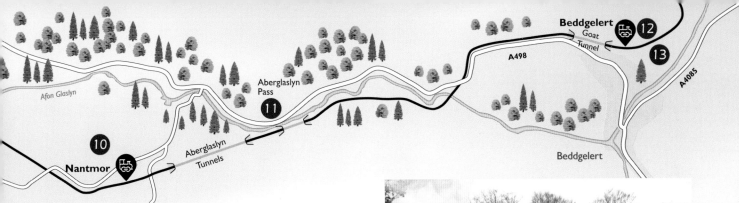

The original station at Beddgelert comprised of two platforms, a passing loop and three sidings and served the original Welsh Highland Railway line during its period of operation from 1922 until 1936. Following the Second World War the line and station were neglected and fell into disrepair, until work to re-build the station, as part of the restoration of the Welsh Highland Railway, commenced in December 2006. The restored station was officially opened by Lord Ellis-Thomas on 7th April 2009.

13 Beddgelert Station Mistress

In 1934 Miriam Roberts was made Station Mistress at Beddgelert, she was 18 at the time. She secured the job for 5 shillings (25p) per week. Her duties, which she always carried out wearing traditional Welsh national costume, included greeting visitors, selling train tickets, postcards and light refreshments. Miriam, who was bilingual and able to speak fluently to passengers in both Welsh and English, was also a valued member of the Eryri Harp Choir and with a beautiful voice was known locally as Llinos Glaslyn – The Glaslyn Linnet.

When the Welsh Highland Railway ceased operations at the end of the 1936 season, Miriam's job was no longer required and she left the station for the final time – although modern-day Station Mistresses Sarah and Rosie, say they sometimes feel her presence as they go about their duties.

Top Right: *Beyer Garratt No. NG130 at Beddgelert Station*
Above inset: *1930s Beddgelert Station Mistress Miriam Roberts*
Below: *Modern-day Beddgelert Station Mistresses Sarah and Rosie*

LLWYBR LLECHI ERYRI – SNOWDONIA SLATE TRAIL

The Llwybr Llechi Eryri – Snowdonia Slate Trail, is an 83-mile (133-km) circular trail established in 2017 which enables walkers to explore the industrial heritage of the North Wales slate industry and its associated villages throughout Snowdonia. https://snowdoniaslatetrail.org/ The route starts at Porth Penrhyn near Bangor and ends at Bethesda in the Nant Ffrancon valley. In between it passes through Llanberis, Waunfawr, Nantlle, Beddgelert, Tanygrisiau, Blaenau Ffestiniog, Betws y Coed and Capel Curig.

Section 7 of the route runs through Beddgelert, the Aberglaslyn Pass, Nantmor and Croesor. You can clearly see the Trail from the Welsh Highland Railway when it is travelling through the Aberglaslyn Pass, as it follows the old Fisherman's Path alongside the Afon Glaslyn, which is located directly below the train line.

The Snowdonia Slate Trail is all part of the move to celebrate North Wales's Slate Industry and bring knowledge of Snowdonia's industrial past to a wider audience.

In recognition of this, in July 2021 the region became a UNESCO World Heritage Site, joining such icons as the Taj Mahal, Grand Canyon and the Egyptian pyramids.

Beddgelert Village

When Prince Arthur Duke of Connaught (son of Queen Victoria and Prince Albert) visited Beddgelert in the late 1870s, this pretty mountain village set amidst the magnificent landscapes of Snowdonia, had already been on the 'tourist trail' for at least a century.

Above: *Beddgelert village and the bridge over the Afon Colwyn .*
Left: *Aberglaslyn by J.M.W. Turner.*
Below: *The Royal Goat Hotel Beddgelert.*

From the 1750s onwards the 'Romantics' in search of the 'sublime and the picturesque' flocked to the area for inspiration, which they channelled into their poetry, prose and art.

In the 1790s both J.M.W. Turner and William Wordsworth visited. Wordsworth's account of climbing Snowdon in 1791 featured in his poem The Prelude and Turner's paintings of nearby Aberglaslyn, inspired thousands more to come and experience 'Wild Wales'.

By the time Prince Arthur visited, the village was already well equipped with several inns, hotels and hostelries. The Prince stayed in The Goat Hotel, which is located immediately below the Welsh Highland Railway line and Beddgelert Station. Following his visit, budding entrepreneur and hotel manager David Prichard renamed the hotel The Royal Goat Hotel.

'The Prelude'
By William Wordsworth (1770–1850)

IT was a close, warm, breezeless summer night,
Wan, dull, and glaring, with a dripping fog
Low-hung and thick that covered all the sky;
But, undiscouraged, we began to climb
The mountain-side. The mist soon girt us round,
And, after ordinary travellers' talk
With our conductor, pensively we sank
Each into commerce with his private thoughts:
Thus did we breast the ascent, and by myself
Was nothing either seen or heard that checked
Those musings or diverted, save that once
The shepherd's lurcher, who, among the crags
Had to his joy unearthed a hedgehog, teased
His coiled-up prey with barkings turbulent.
This small adventure, for even such it seemed
In that wild place and at the dead of night,
Being over and forgotten, on we wound
In silence as before. With forehead bent
Earthward, as if in opposition set
Against an enemy, I panted up

With eager pace, and no less eager thoughts.
Thus might we wear a midnight hour away,
Ascending at loose distance each from each,
And I, as chanced, the foremost of the band;
When at my feet the ground appeared to brighten,
And with a step or two seemed brighter still;
Nor was time given to ask or learn the cause,
For instantly a light upon the turf
Fell like a flash, and lo! as I looked up,
The Moon hung naked in a firmament
Of azure without cloud, and at my feet
Rested a silent sea of hoary mist.
A hundred hills their dusky backs upheaved
All over this still ocean; and beyond,
Far, far beyond, the solid vapours stretched,
In headlands, tongues, and promontory shapes,
Into the main Atlantic, that appeared
To dwindle, and give up his majesty,
Usurped upon far as the sight could reach.

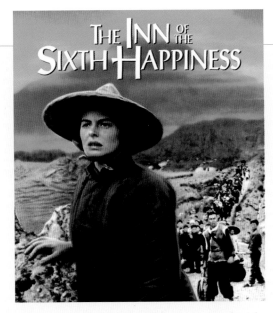

A more recent famous guest to be associated with Beddgelert was Ingrid Bergman, who stayed here during the making of the film The Inn of the Sixth Happiness, which was shot in the mountains surrounding the village, along the Nant Gwynant valley and down the Aberglaslyn Pass where the Afon Glaslyn River was used as the Yellow River in the film!

It was David Pritchard who also promoted the story of the hound Gelert and erected the gravestone near the Afon Glaslyn that draws so many people to Beddgelert today.

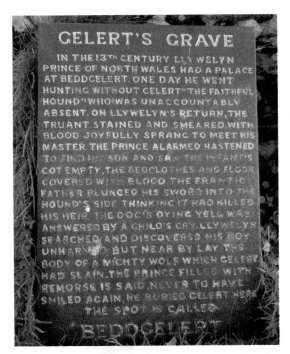

Whilst it is perhaps difficult to separate fact from fiction, this story was most definitely not simply an invention by Pritchard in an attempt to raise the profile of Beddgelert. Written accounts of a hound called 'Cilhart' (Gelert) dying and being buried in the village appear in Welsh literature as early as the 15th century.

However, there is an even earlier account as to why the village may be called Beddgelert (which translates into English as 'the grave of Gelert') and it involves

not a dog but a man. St Mary's Church is located near the centre of Beddgelert close to the meeting point of the Afon Glaslyn and the Afon Colwyn. It is built on the site of an earlier priory which dated back to the sixth century and there is some evidence that it may have been the final resting place of a Celtic Saint from Ireland called Saint Celert who helped spread the Christian faith into Wales.

The oldest surviving building in Beddgelert today is Ty Isaf, a stone cottage which stands alongside the main stone bridge in the village centre. Dating back to the 1600s it is reputed to have been  built on the site of the hunting lodge belonging to the medieval Welsh leader Prince Llewelyn the Great. It is now owned by the National Trust and is well worth a visit to see its oak panelling and large inglenook fireplace. It also houses a small museum and shop.

Another famous person to be associated with Beddgelert was Alfred Bestall MBE, the writer and illustrator of the Rupert the Bear stories, who lived in the village from 1956 until 1985. Originally published as cartoon strips in the Daily Express between 1935 and 1965, the stories were also turned into a series of books which became immensely popular and are still a favourite with children today. One of Alfred Bestall's most famous illustrations entitled 'The Frog Chorus' was the inspiration for a song composed by Sir Paul McCartney called 'We all Stand Together'. The song, along with an animated film, reached Number Three in the UK Singles Chart in 1984. Sir Paul, along with his wife Linda and their children, came to discuss the project with Alfred Bestall in Beddgelert in 1972.

14 Beddgelert Forest

The section of line between Beddgelert and Rhyd Ddu has one of the steepest gradients of any railway in Britain, on average 1 in 40. So, to gain or lose height (depending on the direction of travel) the track follows two large 'S' bends which meander through Beddgelert Forest. The forest which covers 3,000 acres (1214 hectares) is currently managed by Natural Resources Wales, however it was the Forestry Commission (from 1926 onwards) that planted much of the land with the exotic conifer plantations you can see from the train today. This forest was planted on the site of an earlier forest which grew predominantly native oak, birch, and willow. It is now the policy of Natural Resources Wales to gradually fell and reduce the number of conifers in favour of planting more native Welsh trees.

**SAFLE TREFTADAETH Y BYD
Llechi Cymru
Wales Slate
WORLD HERITAGE SITE**

GADER-WYLLT SLATE QUARRY

To the west of Rhyd Ddu Station and clearly visible from the train, is a long causeway which runs to the right-hand side of Llyn y Gader. This causeway once supported a tramway that transported slate from Gader-wyllt Quarry, which is the workings you can see burrowing into the hillside behind the lake.

Gader-wyllt Quarry was operational between 1885 and 1920 and at its peak, in the late 19th century, was producing over one hundred tonnes of dressed slate a year, most of which went to make roofing slates. For every tonne of workable slate, around nine tonnes of waste slate were produced and for a period this waste slate was dumped into the lake! You can still see the remains of this as long, grey coloured 'fingers' stretching out from the shore towards the centre of the lake.

Today, the causeway is part of the Lon Gwyrfai 4½ mile (7.2 Kms) recreational path for walkers, cyclists and horse riders which connects Rhyd Ddu with Beddgelert. It was officially opened in 2013 and forms part of the longer Snowdon Circular Footpath which circumnavigates Wales and England's tallest mountain.

The work of developing the Lon Gwyrfai path was part funded by the Communities and Nature project (CAN), which was a £14.5m European funded project managed by Natural Resources Wales.

Top: *Running left to right, Moel Hebog, Moel yr Ogof and Moel Lefn* (Tony Russell)

Above: *Llyn Llywelyn in Beddgelert Forest* (Tony Russell)

Below Left: *Meillionen Halt* (Tony Russell)

15 Meillionen Halt

There has been a popular camping and caravan site here since the 1950s. Today part of that site has been given over to 16 forest log cabins which can be rented from Forest Holidays **www.forestholidays.co.uk**

At intervals, where the train breaks out from the forest, there are remarkable views in all directions. Immediately to the west lies the dramatic conical outline of Moel Hebog 2,569 feet (783 metres) with its sister peaks of Moel yr Ogof 2,149 feet (655 metres) and Moel Lefyn 2,240 feet (638 metres) alongside. Moel yr Ogof translates from Welsh as 'hill of the cave' and if you look closely you can just make out the entrance to a cave on the facing rocky side of the mountain. In the early part of the 15th century this cave was the hideout for Owain Glyndwr, the last native Welshman to hold the title Prince of Wales and the last person to wage a war of independence against the English.

16 Snowdon

Those travelling on the Welsh Highland Railway between Beddgelert Forest and the village of Rhyd Ddu have the opportunity to enjoy some of the finest views of Snowdon. The summit lies directly to the east of the line and on clear days when the clouds roll away, it is possible to see both the summit cairn and café and the Snowdon Mountain Railway train approaching the summit. At 3,560 feet (1,085 metres) tall, Snowdon is the tallest mountain in both Wales and England. The Welsh name for Snowdon is Yr Wyddfa, which translates as 'the tumulus', 'the barrow' or even 'the tomb'. All three names are said to refer to a legend which states the mountain is the final resting place of a giant killed by King Arthur. Each year around 360,000 people climb to the summit of Snowdon, making it one of the most climbed mountains in the world. Another 250,000 reach the summit on the Snowdon Mountain Railway.

17 Summit Point

Not only can you view the highest place in England and Wales on this stretch of the line, you also pass the summit point of your journey on the Welsh Highland Railway. No matter if you began your journey in Caernarfon or Porthmadog, you would have started by the sea and since then your train has carried you all the way up to Y Copa (The Summit) which is 650 feet (198 metres) above sea level. Given the relatively short distance from each starting point this is a tremendous achievement for the locomotive pulling your train.

The locomotives used on the Welsh Highland Railway are predominantly Beyer Garratt class NG/G16, which are the largest narrow-gauge steam engines in the world and powerful enough to make this epic journey along with up to ten carriages in tow!

18 Pitt's Head Rock

Close to the railway summit point and near where the railway passes through a short tunnel under the A4085 road, is an upright rock known as 'Pitt's Head Rock'. This is due to the fact that its eastern edge is believed to bear a distinct resemblance to the profile of William Pitt the Younger (1759-1806) who became British Prime Minister in 1783 at the young age of 23! There is some suggestion the rock may have been 'improved' to make the likeness more so, but if so, this would have happened more than 140 years ago, as an early photograph of that period shows an identical profile to the one you can see today.

19 Rhyd Ddu Station

The station at Rhyd Ddu marks the half-way point on the Welsh Highland Railway's epic journey from 'coast to coast', Porthmadog to Caernarfon. It is in a beautiful location with 360-degree views of Snowdonia's majestic mountains. From here the Rhyd Ddu footpath up Snowdon begins, taking on average around three to four hours to reach the summit. Many walkers prefer this route to the more popular, busier routes which approach Snowdon from Llanberis and the east. To the west of the station lies the almost circular Llyn y Gader, an isolated glacial lake which often reflects the outline of the Nantlle Ridge located directly behind. It is of great ecological value as it sustains plants and wildlife of national importance such as the Arctic char and Floating water-plantain.

As part of the restoration of the Welsh Highland Railway, Rhyd Ddu Station was constructed in 2003 with additional modifications in 2005/06. The first steam train ran to the station on 28th July 2003 and two days later the station, along with the section of line from Waunfawr to Rhyd Ddu, was officially opened by His Royal Highness the Prince of Wales, who, along with 100 invited guests, travelled to Rhyd Ddu on-board a 'Royal Train'. The train was comprised of three carriages hauled by Ffestiniog Railway's historic locomotive 'Prince' with Prince Charles riding on the footplate between Snowdon Ranger Halt and Rhyd Ddu Station.

Middle Left: *Y Copa (Summit Point) on the Welsh Highland Railway* (David Trout)
Below: *Rhyd Ddu Station* (Roger Dimmick)

Left: *Taking on water at Rhyd Ddu Station*

Right: *Welsh Highland Railway runs alongside Llyn Cwellyn*

Bottom Left: *Cwellyn Arms in Rhyd Ddu*

Bottom right: *Llyn Cwellyn with Mynydd Mawr in the background*

20 Rhyd Ddu Village

The village of Rhyd Ddu lies just to the north of Rhyd Ddu Station. Its Welsh name translates into English as 'black ford' and the village would have originally grown up around the crossing point of the nearby Afon Gwyrfai River. The village is located at the meeting point of three valleys, the Colwyn valley leading south to Beddgelert, the Nantlle valley leading west to Penygroes and the Afon Gwyrfai valley leading north towards Caernarfon. Originally a small farming community, the population of Rhyd Ddu increased substantially during the second half of the 19th century due to the opening up of several slate quarries and copper mines within the vicinity. Today the village is on the tourist trail and becoming increasingly popular as a base for walkers and climbers to the area. The Cwellyn Arms www.snowdoninn.co.uk provides great food and comfortable overnight accommodation from traditional B & B to bunkhouse-style. Meanwhile, if it's a special cup of Dutch coffee that appeals, or some home-made Welsh cakes, then you should visit Emma and Menno at Ty Mawr Tea Rooms and B & B **www.snowdonaccomodation.co.uk**

21 Llyn Cwellyn

As the line begins to curve around a long 'horseshoe' bend, the train passes several attractive old Welsh farms, these are predominantly mountain sheep farms, although some cattle will be grazed on the lower slopes. From here there are superb views to the west across the valley and Llyn Cwellyn to the forested lower slopes of Mynydd Mawr (Big Mountain) beyond. Although now used as a reservoir, Llyn Cwellyn is a natural glacial lake formed at the end of the last Ice Age some 12,000 years ago. It has an area of 215 acres (87 hectares) and is very deep at 120 feet (37 metres), consequently it is one of just a handful of lakes in Wales to support a natural population of Arctic char. It is also home to brown trout and otters are frequently seen at its northern end.

22 Mynydd Mawr

Mynydd Mawr, the large mountain rising to a height of 2,290 feet (698 metres) immediately above Llyn Cwellyn, is known locally as 'Yr Eliffant' (The Elephant) as its profile is often thought to resemble an elephant lying down and drinking from the lake. On the higher slopes of the mountain you can still find remnants of wreckage from two planes which unfortunately crashed here in bad weather. The first was a De Havilland 'Mosquito' which crashed in 1944 during World War II and the second a 'Vampire' jet which crashed in 1956.

23 Glan-Yr-Afon

Just to the south of Snowdon Ranger Halt the line turns sharply as it crosses the magnificent Glan-yr-afon 'viaduct'. This bridge (for in essence that is what it is) was built around 1880 and is nearly 100 feet (30.48 metres) long and has a span of 94 feet (28.6 metres) across the Afon Treweunyd far below. Immediately to the east of the line at this point and partially hidden amongst trees, are a series of spectacular waterfalls, the waters from which cascade down beneath the railway line before flowing on into Llyn Cwellyn.

Left: *Glan-yr-Afon viaduct*
Right: *Snowdon Ranger Youth Hostel*

24 Snowdon Ranger Halt

Snowdon Ranger Halt is located close to the Snowdon Ranger Youth Hostel, which was originally a tavern with accommodation called the Saracen's Head Inn. The name 'Snowdon Ranger' derives from John Morton, former owner of the Inn, who also fulfilled the role of mountain guide, escorting Victorian adventurers staying in the hotel, to the summit of Snowdon from this point. His trail up Snowdon, which is believed to be the oldest path to the summit, is known today as The Snowdon Ranger Path and is a popular route for present-day walkers. There is also a footpath to Llanberis which starts here.

SAFLE TREFTADAETH Y BYD
**Llechi Cymru
Wales Slate**
WORLD HERITAGE SITE

GLANRAFON SLATE QUARRY

Between Rhyd Ddu and Snowdon Ranger Halt the Welsh Highland Railway winds its way through some of the finest scenery in the whole of Snowdonia. Immediately north of Rhyd Ddu, on the lower slopes of Snowdon itself, are the remains of Glanrafon Slate Quarry.

Up until the 1870s quarrying here was on a small scale, but with the coming of the original Welsh Highland Railway (known simply then as the North Wales Narrow Gauge Railways) production increased dramatically and in 1882 the quarry employed close on 100 men and produced 1725 tons of finished slate.

The waste slate from this production can be seen piled on the mountainsides today.

Yr Wyddfa
Snowdon

One of the highlights of any trip on the Welsh Highland Railway is the opportunity to experience spectacular views of Snowdon from several different angles and on clear days it is even possible to see the summit cairn and café from the train!

At 3,560 feet (1,085 metres) above sea-level, Snowdon is taller than any other mountain in both England and Wales and is also the most climbed mountain in the world. Each year around 360,000 people climb to the summit of Snowdon, the majority using one of seven recognised routes which approach the mountain from all points of the compass and a further 250,000 reach the summit on the Snowdon Mountain Railway **www.snowdonrailway.co.uk**

Views of Snowdon can be obtained from Porthmadog without even leaving Harbour Station! All you need to do is walk along the platform towards the signal box and then look north. As you walk further away from the station more and more of the mountains surrounding Snowdon are revealed and, if you look in the opposite

direction, there are views of the little seaside village and sandy bays of Borth y Gest (a great walk from Harbour Station) with the open sea beyond.

Once on the Welsh Highland Railway there are three points on your journey where Snowdon comes into view and all offer something different. These are between the stations of Pont Croesor and Nantmor (see pages 8 – 9), between the stations of Beddgelert and Rhyd Ddu (see pages 14 – 15) and between the stations of Rhyd Ddu and Snowdon Ranger (see pages 20 – 21).

Top: *Hafod Eryri on top of Yr Wyddfa (Snowdon)* (Snowdon Mountain Railway)

Middle: *The Snowdon Summit Hotel Circa 1880s*

Below: *Yr Wyddfa (Snowdon) from the Welsh Highland Railway near Snowdon Ranger*

SNOWDON IN LEGEND

The Welsh name for Snowdon is Yr Wyddfa, which translates as 'the tumulus', 'the barrow' or even 'the tomb'. All three names are said to refer to the final resting place of a giant of a man called Rhita (Rhudda Gawr) who had conquered all the kings of Britain except for one – King Arthur. Rhita challenged Arthur to a sword fight on a mountain, which is identified by early storytellers as being Snowdon. Arthur won the fight and Rhita was buried by King Arthur's knights on the summit with a massive pile of rocks heaped over the body – thereby creating a cairn.

SNOWDON IN FACT

We will never know how much truth there may be in the King Arthur legend, however it is true to say there was a large cairn of rocks on the summit until the early 1800s. After that, some of the rocks were used to build a summit 'tower' and then for the walls of a refreshment hut for walkers which was built soon after 1815. A summit cairn of rocks was rebuilt by the Royal Engineers in 1827 whilst they were surveying the mountain, and this was further enlarged in 1841. Throughout the latter half of the 19th century more huts were built on the summit becoming collectively known by the rather grand title of 'The Snowdon Summit Hotel'. The construction and opening of the Snowdon Mountain Railway line in 1895-1896 brought

further infrastructure to the summit with the building of a summit station.

In the 20th century as hiking became an ever-increasing popular pastime, more and more people ascended Snowdon and with them came more and more criticism for the 'hotch potch' of buildings around the summit. In response to this Sir Clough Williams-Ellis (creator of Portmeirion) was commissioned to design one single building which would fulfil all requirements – summit station, visitor centre, shelter and refreshments. This new building opened in 1934 and all other summit buildings were removed. Sadly Sir Clough's talents for flamboyant attractive architectural design were never given full rein on this project (he himself complained of too little time and money with too many restrictions to produce something worthy of the highest summit in England and Wales) and what resulted was a rather mundane concrete box with a flat roof, which was later referred to by His Royal Highness The Prince of Wales as being 'a carbuncle on the mountain' and 'the highest slum in England and Wales'.

By the beginning of 2000, it was clear this building needed to be replaced and work began shortly afterwards to raise the necessary funds. This was achieved and by 2009 Sir Clough's building had been demolished and the current visitor centre named Hafod Eryri (Snowdon summer residence), was opened to much positive comment. Built from granite it sits comfortably below the summit cairn where it withstands windspeeds in excess of 150 mph (241 kms per hour), over 197 inches (5 metres) of precipitation each year and temperatures below minus 20 degrees centigrade. Outside the winter season it also withstands the footfall and walking boots of many thousands of visitors.

Top: *Snowdon Mountain Railway*
(Snowdon Mountain Railway)

Left: *Snowdon summit cairn Circa 1860s*

27 Cefn-Du and Moel Eilio

Just south of Waunfawr there are fine views of the mountains to the east of the line including Cefn-du 1,447 feet (441 metres) and Moel Eilio 2,382 feet (726 metres). Moel Eilio is the most northerly outlier of Snowdon's satellites from which it is possible to walk south along the ridgeline onto Snowdon itself. On Moel Eilio's western flank there are a series of adits (mine entrances) which appear like a fault line running up the mountain. They are particularly visible in the afternoon when lit up by the sun as it sinks towards the west. Cefn-du is probably best known as being the location for Marconi's radio transmission station. In 1913 the Italian wireless pioneer opened Britain's first long-wave wireless transmitting station here and it proved to be a vital tool in the First World War enabling Britain to communicate with allied ships in the North Atlantic. The station closed in 1938 but remnants of foundations of buildings and masts still exist on the top today.

25 Afon Gwyrfai

Between Snowdon Ranger and Waunfawr the line of the Welsh Highland Railway follows the course of the fast-running and very beautiful Afon Gwyrfai, crossing and re-crossing the river in several places. Afon Gwyrfai roughly translates into English as 'the river that falls' and for the beginning of its journey to the sea it does just that, springing from the mountains high above Rhyd Ddu, before dropping quickly to that village and heading northwards through Llyn Cwellyn to Waunfawr, where it turns west and flows out to the Menai Strait just to the west of Caernarfon.

26 Plas y Nant Halt

Plas y Nant Halt is situated alongside the Afon Gwyrfai and close to a flood control weir (clearly visible from the train) managed by the National River Authority. A halt was first built here in the 1920s but became disused following the closure of the original North Wales Narrow Gauge Railways line in 1936. This new halt was built from funds raised by the Friends of Plas y Nant and opened on May 15th 2005. Plas y Nant once was an outdoor-pursuits centre and lies to the east of the line and is clearly visible from the train.

Top: *Beyer Garratt NGG16 No. 87 crossing the Afon Gwyrfai* (Roger Dimmick)

Middle: *St Garmon's Church in Betws Garmon* (Roy Woods)

Below: *The WHR line runs alongside the Afon Gwyrfai near Plas y Nant* (David Thurlow)

28 Betws Garmon Church

The attractive church at Betws Garmon is dedicated to Saint Garmon who was a Gallican bishop who came to Britain around 470 AD to help bring Christianity to North Wales. He established schools in the region for the Christian instruction of young people and it is believed one of these schools was at Betws Garmon. The present Church was built in 1841-2 on the site of an earlier church but to a different alignment. This can be seen from the positioning of the gravestones. The western end of the earlier church was where the chancel is today and it pointed away from the road towards the north. Close to the Church is the northern boundary of the Snowdonia National Park.

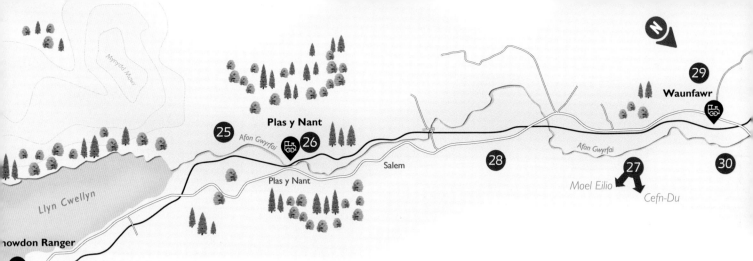

30 Snowdonia Parc Brewpub

The Snowdonia Parc Brewpub is located in what used to be Waunfawr Station Master's house prior to the original station closure in 1936. Today you can watch the passing trains whilst enjoying lunch or a drink in the beer garden! There is a microbrewery on site which brews several award-winning real ales. Carman Pierce, the pub owner and brewer, was awarded the CAMRA Gwynedd & Mon 'Pub of the Year' for four consecutive years from 2012 until 2015.

Left: *The Snowdonia Parc Brewpub by Waunfawr Station*
Below Left: *Waunfaw Station (Chris Parry)*

29 Waunfawr Station

The first station at Waunfawr was built for the North Wales Narrow Gauge Railways in 1877 and it was the principal passing point on the NWNGR for trains transporting slate from the quarries around Rhyd Ddu to Dinas Junction. From Dinas the slate could be transferred onto the London and North Western standard gauge rail network. Waunfawr station was abandoned in 1936 when the line was closed but reopened as part of the restoration of the Welsh Highland Railway line in August 2000. The present-day station consists of an island platform with a high-level footbridge linking it to a car park and the Snowdonia Parc Brewpub on one side of the railway and a campsite on the other. During the winter of 2018/2019 a new station building, in the traditional style of the NWNGR, was built on the platform. The building was officially opened by the Right Honourable Lord Dafydd Wigley on 14th June 2019. Of particular note here are the colourful island flowerbeds positioned along the platform. These are all maintained by staff and volunteers working for the Welsh Highland Railway.

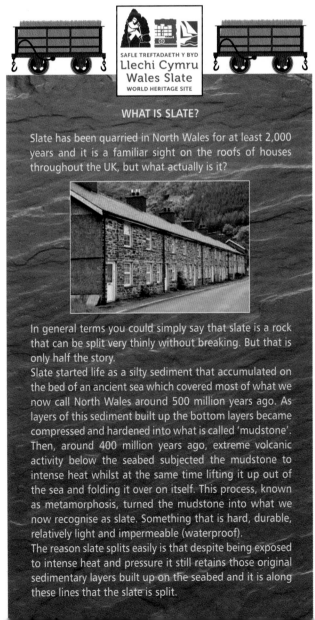

SAFLE TREFTADAETH Y BYD
Llechi Cymru
Wales Slate
WORLD HERITAGE SITE

WHAT IS SLATE?

Slate has been quarried in North Wales for at least 2,000 years and it is a familiar sight on the roofs of houses throughout the UK, but what actually is it?

In general terms you could simply say that slate is a rock that can be split very thinly without breaking. But that is only half the story.

Slate started life as a silty sediment that accumulated on the bed of an ancient sea which covered most of what we now call North Wales around 500 million years ago. As layers of this sediment built up the bottom layers became compressed and hardened into what is called 'mudstone'. Then, around 400 million years ago, extreme volcanic activity below the seabed subjected the mudstone to intense heat whilst at the same time lifting it up out of the sea and folding it over on itself. This process, known as metamorphosis, turned the mudstone into what we now recognise as slate. Something that is hard, durable, relatively light and impermeable (waterproof).

The reason slate splits easily is that despite being exposed to intense heat and pressure it still retains those original sedimentary layers built up on the seabed and it is along these lines that the slate is split.

Above: *Waunfawr Station*

Top Right: *Restoration of Tryfan Junction Station building was completed in 2014*

31 Waunfawr

The village of Waunfawr is approximately a ten-minute walk from the Station. It straddles the A4085 Beddgelert to Caernarfon road in an open, elevated position with far-reaching views west to the Irish Sea and north-west to the town of Caernarfon, Menai Strait and Anglesey (Ynys Mon) beyond. The name 'Waunfawr' translates to English as 'big mountain pasture' and reflects the mountainous open grazing land which surrounds the village. The village (and Anglesey) are both visible from the train when travelling this section of the line from Waunfawr Station to Tryfan Junction.

32 Tryfan Junction

Tryfan Junction is unique being the only station located at a narrow-gauge railway junction in the UK. Today it is a quiet request halt on the Welsh Highland Railway, however, during the period from 1877 until 1936 it was a busy interchange between the two North Wales Narrow Gauge Railways lines, one running to the slate quarries near Rhyd Ddu and the other to Bryngwyn and the slate quarries on Moel Tryfan. Following the closure of these lines in 1936 Tryfan Junction station fell into complete disrepair until a

group of railway enthusiasts from the Welsh Highland Heritage Group began the task of restoration in 2009. Restoration of the station building you can see today was completed in 2014.

SAFLE TREFTADAETH Y BYD
Llechi Cymru
Wales Slate
WORLD HERITAGE SITE

SLATE TRAIL - LLWYBR LLECHI

As well as the WHR train you are travelling on, the recently created Llwybr Llechi Slate Trail also passes through Tryfan Junction and then follows the original track bed of the old North Wales Narrow Gauge Railways branch-line to Bryngwyn, which was used to transport slate away from the Moel Tryfan, Alexandra and Cilgwyn quarries.

En route the Slate Trail passes through the villages of Rhostryfan and Rhosgadfan, both of which have far-reaching views westwards to Anglesey and the Irish Sea beyond. Many of the houses within these villages were built in the 19th century for the families of men working in the nearby quarries. At its peak in 1862 the Alexandra Quarry alone employed over 200 workers.

Cilgwyn holds the distinction of being one of the longest working slate quarries in Great Britain, having been worked from the 12th century right through until its closure in 1956. It is said that slate from Cilgwyn Quarry was used in the construction of Caernarfon Castle for King Edward 1st in the 13th century.

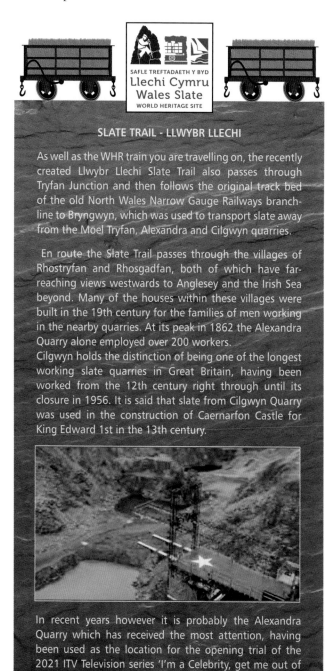

In recent years however it is probably the Alexandra Quarry which has received the most attention, having been used as the location for the opening trial of the 2021 ITV Television series 'I'm a Celebrity, get me out of Here!' which was watched by an audience of over eight million!

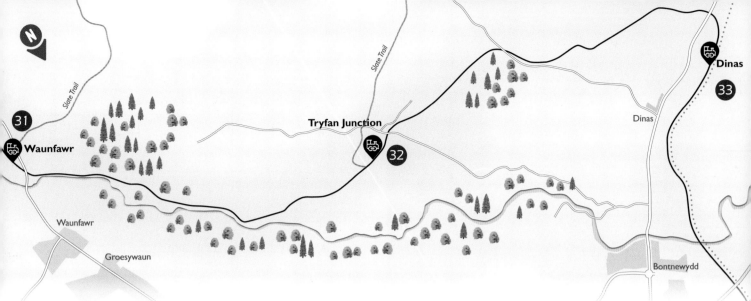

33 Dinas

Dinas Junction was originally opened in 1877 as the transfer point of slate quarried near Rhyd Ddu and Moel Tryfan from the North Wales Narrow Gauge Railways network to the standard gauge London and North Western mainline. Narrow gauge passenger trains ceased operating through Dinas in 1936 and the standard gauge mainline closed in 1964 as part of the 'Beeching cuts'.

As part of the restoration of the Welsh Highland Railway line out of Caernarfon, Dinas station re-opened

on 11 October 1997 and was temporarily the southern terminus before further restoration work took the line to Waunfawr in 2000. The new narrow-gauge platforms at Dinas are built on the site of the former standard gauge platforms. Two buildings survive from the North Wales Narrow Gauge Railways era, namely the former goods shed and the original station building which has been carefully restored. Dinas is the main locomotive depot and engineering works for the Welsh Highland Railway, along with Boston Lodge near Porthmadog which also services the Ffestiniog Railway. Trains often stop at Dinas for a few minutes whilst the locomotive takes on coal. It may be possible to alight from your train at this point to watch this operation.

Above Right: *Beyer Garratts NGG16 No.87 & K1 at Dinas* (David Trout)
Middle: *Dinas Junction in the early 1930s*
Below: *Hunslet 'ladies'. Linda and Blanche, 'double heading' at Dinas*

Above: *Lon Efion cycle route*
Right: *Yr Eifl (The Rivals) from Trefor* (Tony Russell)
Bottom Right: *Ynys Llanddwyn* (Tony Russell)

34 Lôn Eifion

Between Dinas Station and Caernarfon the Welsh Highland Railway runs alongside a section of the old standard gauge London and North Western line which operated until 1964 between Caernarfon and Afon Wen - situated on the south coast of the Llyn Peninsula. Today, the track bed is used for the Lôn Eifion cycle route which is a section of the Lôn Las Cymru, Welsh National Cycle Route (NCR 8) that runs from Cardiff to Holyhead covering a distance of approximately 250 miles (400 kilometres).

35 Ynys Llanddwyn - Llanddwyn Island

To the north of Dinas there are fine views from the train to Anglesey and in particular Llanddwyn Island, a small tidal island which can be accessed at low tide from the beach near Newborough Forest. Dwynwen is the Welsh Patron Saint of Lovers, making her the Welsh equivalent of St. Valentine. Her Saint's Day is 25th January and is often celebrated in Wales with the gifting of cards and flowers. The island bears the ruined remains of St Dwynwen's Church and Twr Mawr lighthouse, which is built in the style of the old windmills which at one time were common on Anglesey. The lighthouse marks the western approach to the Menai Strait. Llanddwyn Island was used as the location for the BBC One TV series 'The 1900 Island' which was screened during May 2019.

36 Bontnewydd Halt

Bontnewydd (meaning new bridge) is a request halt two miles south of Caernarfon which was re-opened on 31st May 1999 as part of Phase One of the restoration project to re-build the Welsh Highland Railway. Prior to the re-opening of Bontnewydd halt, which has no station buildings and a single low platform, there was a petition for its re-opening signed by local residents. Just south of the halt is a fine three-arched viaduct over the Afon Gwyrfai which was designed in 1867 by C. E. Spooner, son of James Spooner who, amongst many other things, surveyed the original line for the Ffestiniog Railway.

37 Yr Eifl 'The Rivals'

Just south of Caernarfon there are spectacular views from the train towards the south-west and Yr Eifl 'The Rivals', a three-peaked mountain on the north coast of the Llyn Peninsula. The Rivals rise from sea-level at Nant Gwrtheyrn to 1,841 feet (561 metres) at the top of the central peak. There is a radio relay station on the peak nearest the sea as well as a quarry lower down, which produced granite setts (kerb stones) until its closure in 1963, however granite from the

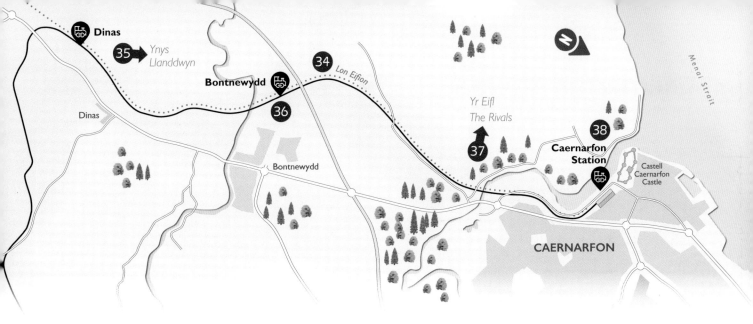

quarry was used to produce the curling stones used in the Winter Olympics held in Turin, Italy in 2006. The third and smallest peak (Tre Ceri) has on its summit one of the best preserved, most densely occupied hill forts in Britain, which was continuously occupied from the Bronze Age through to the Romano-British period (AD 50-400). Archaeologists believe that at one time the hill fort had as many as 400 inhabitants.

38 Caernarfon Station

On the outskirts of Caernarfon the train passes through Fron Goch Garden Centre and Nursery, which is always worth a visit if you have a garden, or enjoy plants. The line also follows the eastern bank of Afon Seiont where there are magnificent views of Caernarfon Castle (see pages 34-37). The Menai Strait and Anglesey beyond are the backdrop to boats at berth on the river with the Ffestiniog and Welsh Highland Railway's new modern-design Caernarfon Station in the foreground (see pages 26-27).

Right: *Entrance to the new Caernarfon Station*
Below: *Caernarfon Station and Caernarfon Castle alongside the Afon Seiont*

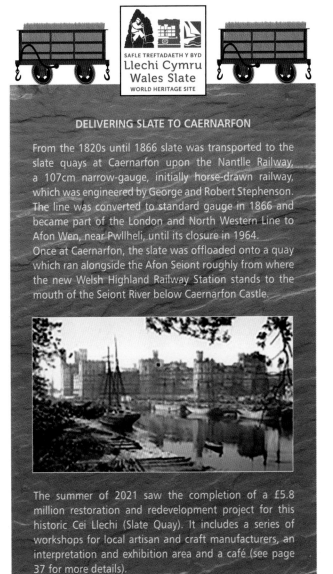

DELIVERING SLATE TO CAERNARFON

From the 1820s until 1866 slate was transported to the slate quays at Caernarfon upon the Nantlle Railway, a 107cm narrow-gauge, initially horse-drawn railway, which was engineered by George and Robert Stephenson. The line was converted to standard gauge in 1866 and became part of the London and North Western Line to Afon Wen, near Pwllheli, until its closure in 1964.

Once at Caernarfon, the slate was offloaded onto a quay which ran alongside the Afon Seiont roughly from where the new Welsh Highland Railway Station stands to the mouth of the Seiont River below Caernarfon Castle.

The summer of 2021 saw the completion of a £5.8 million restoration and redevelopment project for this historic Cei Llechi (Slate Quay). It includes a series of workshops for local artisan and craft manufacturers, an interpretation and exhibition area and a café (see page 37 for more details).

Caernarfon Station

The Welsh Highland Railway now has a stunning new £3 million railway station at Caernarfon. This station not only provides a gateway to the Welsh Highland Railway but also includes a shop, exhibition hall and great coffee shop which offers panoramic views of Caernarfon's World Heritage Castle and the adjacent Waterfront. `

The original 19th century Welsh Highland Railway never ran as far as Caernarfon, the terminus was at Dinas, located a few miles south of Caernarfon, where there was a large interchange site with the standard-gauge London & North Western Railway. However, when the railway was being reconstructed in the 1990s, it made sense to start from the 'Royal Town' and its UNESCO World Heritage castle, which was already a tourist hub.

The new stretch of line followed the route of the long-closed London & North Western Railway, which used to continue through a tunnel under the town (now used for a road) and on to a station on the north side - where Morrison's supermarket now stands. The new station, therefore, had to be on the south side of the tunnel in a run down and almost forgotten area beside the river with many derelict buildings around it.

But this was not always the case. This site was once a thriving hub with quays along both sides of the Afon Seiont River. The Caernarfon Harbour Trust was formed back in 1793 to manage the area. The Nantlle tramway brought slate to the quays to be stacked and taken away by sailing ships and many other related businesses grew up alongside. The big wall that backs the new station was constructed in the early 1800's to widen the quays and give extra space for this expanding hive of industry.

In 1997 the Welsh Highland Railway put in their first station in Caernarfon, which consisted of a small porta-cabin for ticket sales. Other temporary arrangements followed, latterly including a booking office and large shop with adjacent toilets. This makeshift station was not befitting for a terminus station of a world class attraction, but hemmed in between the road and the great wall, it was not an easy site to develop, so although there was a desire to have something better, it would need both vision and money to create. Thus, it continued to serve the railway in this form for 20 years, only closing in 2017 to make way for the exciting 21st century architecturally designed and improved terminus.

Opened in 2019, the Station has been beautifully designed to complement but not compete with its medieval neighbour. With its sleek sinuous lines and clever use of glass, metal and stone the Station is a triumphant testament to the hard work and resolve displayed by all partners involved. It also forms a key part to Caernarfon's £16 million Waterfront Regeneration Project, which has been led by Gwynedd County Council and part funded by the European

Above Right: *Modern new station* (Gwynn Jones)

Below: *View from the castle in 1904 clearly shows the station site beneath the retaining wall. Note the Harbour Trust offices and the neat stacks of slate awaiting transportation from this busy river scene.* (Gwynedd Archives Service)

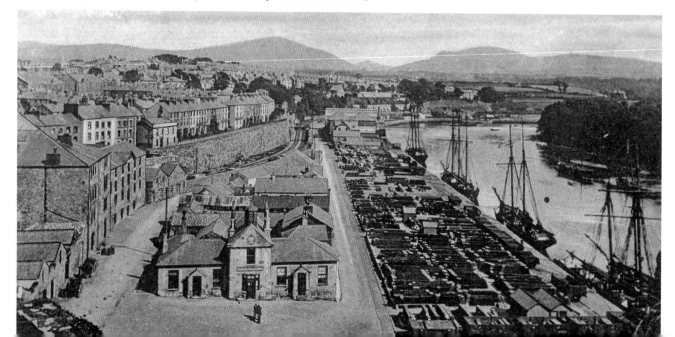

Regional Development Fund through the Welsh Government.

The first steps towards the creation of Caernarfon's new station took place in 2013 with the launch of an architectural design competition. Seven designs were submitted to a panel of judges which included representatives from the Ffestiniog & Welsh Highland Railways, the Welsh Government and Gwynedd County Council. Other independent advisors that became involved in final design discussions included CADW and the Caernarfon Harbour Trust. All parties agreed the design should sit comfortably alongside the nearby World Heritage site of Caernarfon Castle but make its own statement and not be a 'mock castle, nor a Victorian pastiche'.

The eventual winners of the competition were Purcell, a renowned international architectural company who also designed the award-winning visitor centre for Yr Ysgwrn, Snowdonia home of Welsh bard and First World War poet Hedd Wynn.

Stations are all about a sense of arrival, be it at the beginning of a journey or the end. For those excitedly arriving at Caernarfon station ready to commence their journey on the Welsh Highland Railway, the sense of arrival begins in the station's welcome rotunda. In this bright and modern space there is a nod back to times past as it is home to a curious little 'coffeepot' style locomotive, built by the De Winton Ironworks, just across the road. It is here you are met by our host who will direct you to check in after which you are free to explore the shop, check out the event space and collect your hamper. Or you may wish to visit the café, Caffi De Winton, where you can gaze over Caernarfon's magnificent Castle, the new Cei Llechi development and adjacent waterfront.

For those who arrive at Caernarfon Station on a Welsh Highland Railway steam train, the new station is your launch pad to a fascinating and enjoyable visit to one of the world's finest castles, the bustling medieval town of Caernarfon and its network of footpaths, some of which follow the water's edge of the Menai Strait and afford glorious views of the Isle of Anglesey (Ynys Môn) beyond.

The once run-down quayside beneath the castle is now starting to thrive again, with Caernarfon's new railway station sitting proudly at its heart.

Left: *Coffee overlooking Cei llechi and the castle from the mezzanine floor of Caffi De Winton.* (Sara Jackson)

Below: *Watching the train leave from the large and airy event space.* (Gwynn Jones)

Bottom: *A modern view shows the station nestled below the old retaining wall.* (Gwynn Jones)

Above: *NGG16 **No.130** awaits departure from Caernarfon with the Gelert Explorer Service.* (David Trout)

Below: *NGG16 **No.138** leaves the Aberglaslyn Pass over Bryn y Felin bridge; a popular spot for watching the trains.* (David Trout)

Volunteer fireman Cedric Lodge fills the water tank of K1, the world's first Garratt locomotive, which is much smaller than it's younger cousins so needs water more often. (John Ellis Williams)

Caernarfon and its Surroundings

In 1986 Caernarfon was added to the UNESCO list of World Heritage Sites under the title 'The Castles and Town Walls of King Edward I in Gwynedd'. The listing was made in recognition of Caernarfon's global importance and the need to conserve its unique historical sites for future generations to visit, study and enjoy.

Caernarfon Castle

In the late 11th century William the Conqueror ordered the construction of a motte-and-bailey castle at Caernarfon as part of his Norman invasion of Wales. His invasion failed and Wales remained an independent nation until 1283, when Edward I conquered Wales and began to build a series of powerful castles to reduce the risk of future Welsh rebellion. The most imposing of these castles is Caernarfon and Edward I also founded a walled town immediately outside the Castle walls as well as a quay alongside the Menai Strait.

Caernarfon's symbolic status as the most important English stronghold in Wales was secured when the last Welsh Prince of Wales Llewelyn ap Gruffudd was killed in battle by Edward I and the King invested his own son Edward II (who was actually born in Caernarfon in 1284) as the new 'Prince of Wales'.

Today, Caernarfon Castle is probably one of the most famous castles in the world. It was here in 1969 that the Investiture of Prince Charles as Prince of Wales took place. That event was watched by 19 million people on UK TV and an estimated further 500 million worldwide. In late 2019 the adaptation of the same event within the Netflix TV series The Crown (which was also filmed in Caernarfon) has so far drawn an audience of 29 million and introduced a whole new generation to Caernarfon and the surrounding North Wales region.

Above: *The Investiture of HRH The Prince of Wales in Caernarfon Castle in 1969* (BBC Archives)
Bottom: *Caernarfon Castle* (Roger Dimmick)

Caernarfon Castle is just a five-minute walk from the WHR's Caernarfon Station and can even be viewed from the Station café! The Castle is managed by Cadw and open to the public all year round. From its battlements and towers there are magnificent views over the Menai Strait, Isle of Anglesey and the mountains of Snowdonia. Within the Castle there are exhibitions, films and photographs on past Welsh Princes and the Investiture of Prince Charles as the Prince of Wales in 1969. The Castle also contains the Regimental Museum of the Royal Welch Fusiliers.

For further information visit **www.cadw.gov.wales**

Caernarfon Town

A vibrant town has grown up around Caernarfon Castle, both within the old town walls and alongside the Afon Seiont River and the Menai Strait. At the very centre of the town is Y Maes (The Square) an open, semi-pedestrianised piazza which shelters beneath the castle walls and is surrounded by shops, pubs (including Bar Bach the smallest bar in Wales) and cafes, some with al fresco tables, seating and umbrellas, giving Y Maes a slightly Mediterranean feel, especially on market day and when the sun is shining!

It is worth strolling across Y Maes to admire the statue of Lloyd George, to this day the only British Prime Minister to have lived most of his life in Wales (he was Liberal MP for Caernarvon Borough (sic.) from 1890 until 1945) and to have spoken Welsh as his first language.

Lloyd George is widely considered to have been one of the top three British Prime Ministers of the 20th century and is credited with laying the foundations for the modern welfare state. During his tenure he supported the introduction of state pensions, introduced state financial support for the sick and the infirm and brought in National Insurance and unemployment insurance.

Off Y Maes are a number of narrow streets lined with interesting shops to explore, including colourful Palace Street, which triumphed in the 2019 Great British High Street Awards, winning the Best in Wales award as well as being shortlisted for the Best High Street in the UK award. Located nearby is The Black Boy Inn a fascinating traditional old maritime hostelry which was built in 1522 and is one of the oldest inns in Wales.

Above: *Caernarfon's old streets are often filled with colour. Here, umbrellas adorn Palace Street* (Gwynedd Council)

Left: *Café culture on Y Maes gives the town square a continental feel* (Gwynedd Council)

Below: *Intriguing Hole in the wall Street* (Roy Woods)

The annual food festival, 'Gwyl Fwyd Caernarfon' is one of several events held during the year when the whole town comes to life. The area enjoys a wide selection of local food and craft producers and this is a great showcase for them. Caernarfon Station are proud to play their part in local events bringing new people to the railway.

Doc Fictoria

It is a short walk from Y Maes to Caernarfon's dock and harbour area, known as Doc Fictoria (Victoria Dock). Until recently this was a neglected part of Caernarfon, but not so now. In recent years it has benefited from a £16 million Waterfront Regeneration Project, which has been led by Gwynedd County Council and part funded by the European Regional Development Fund through the Welsh Government. Here alongside the Menai Strait you will find a theatre and cinema complex, shops, hotels, bars and restaurants where you can sit and watch the yachts entering and leaving Caernarfon Marina.

The All Wales Coast Path

The All Wales Coast Path is 870 miles (1,400 km) long. It was officially opened on 5th May 2012 and follows (or runs close to) the entire coastline of Wales. The Footpath passes alongside the Castle and can be followed eastwards past Doc Fictoria and alongside the Menai Strait, or westwards across Afon Seiont River via the swing bridge and towards Abermenai Point and Fort Belan.
www.walescoastpath.gov.uk

Cei Llechi

Another fascinating project that has benefitted from the Waterfront Regeneration Project is Cei Llechi. Once part of the harbour's industrial hub, this group of buildings on what is known as the 'Island Site' had fallen into dereliction. All apart from the stoic Harbour Trust Office which remained in use. Over the past few years, some buildings have been repaired while others have been carefully replaced, giving an eclectic mix of shape and colour. The old forge has been recovered and a local blacksmith is proud to be using it once again. The site is now home to many small artisan businesses and a great place to explore. Outside, an old salmon fishing boat has been turned into a most unusual seat – a reminder of the areas maritime past.

Menai cruises

Forged & Pressed at Cei Llechi

At Cei Llechi artisan blacksmiths Chris and Bethan Mace are reopening the doors of what was once the Brunswick Ironworks of the artist blacksmith D J Williams, who originally established his ironworks on this site more than a century ago in 1906.

Chris and Bethan are relighting the forge as part of their mission to make blacksmithing accessible to the public. Visitors to their works can take the opportunity to wander through the courtyard garden and look through the doors and immerse themselves in the sensory experience of forging. The heat of the fire, the sound of hammer on metal, the sight of hot metal being wrought by the smith.

Visitors will be able to see the many techniques used by the smith to forge ironwork for the garden, for cooking over fire and a thousand other uses.

Menai Strait Cruises

One of the best ways of viewing Caernarfon Castle, Anglesey and the Menai Strait is from the deck of 'The Queen of the Sea', a pleasure boat which is moored on the Afon Seiont River alongside the Castle and car park. Offering 40 minute and two-hour cruises from April until October (weather permitting) Emrys the Menai Strait Pilot, will tell you all about Caernarfon and the surrounding area during your cruise and will point out Ynys Llanddwyn Island the location for the BBC One TV series 'The 1900 Island' which was screened during May 2019. **www.menaicruises.co.uk**

Top of page: *Cei Llechi's restored buildings add to Caernarfon's colourful presence* (Chris Parry)
Left: *Salmon boat* (Clare Britton)

Blacksmith's Forge
(Chris Mace)

Porthmadog and its Surroundings

Before William Madocks constructed the mile-long (1.6 kms) sea wall (known as The Cob) across the tidal estuary of Traeth Mawr in 1811, the town of Porthmadog did not exist. The Cob's construction diverted the course of the River Glaslyn, squeezing it through sluice gates at the western end of the embankment. At the release point beyond the gates, such was the water's power that it scoured out a deep channel. It did not take Madocks long to realise the potential of such a channel and soon he had established the beginnings of Porthmadog Harbour alongside the channel. By 1825 it was a flourishing port and the town of Porthmadog was fast developing alongside, to house and service the port workers and their families. Today Porthmadog is a vibrant town which attracts thousands of holidaymakers each year, many drawn to the area by the Ffestiniog & Welsh Highland Railways and the town's proximity to a beautiful coastline and the mountains of Snowdonia.

Porthmadog Harbour Station

The railway station at the western end of The Cob (Harbour Station) was originally built as the terminus for slate being transported by rail from the quarries in the mountains around Ffestiniog to ships berthed at the nearby harbour. The station opened to passengers on 6th January 1865 and continued to offer a passenger service until the outbreak of the Second World War, closing on 15th September 1939. During the war the station buildings were used as the headquarters and billet of Dutch Commandos. A memorial plaque in Spooner's café commemorates this event. The station re-opened to passengers on 23rd July 1955 and has been in operation ever since. In 2011 Harbour

Station also became the departure point for the newly restored Welsh Highland Railway and in March 2014 a £1.1 million project was completed which allowed trains from both the Ffestiniog and the Welsh Highland Railways to be at station platforms at the same time.

Ballast Island

The little island visible (but not accessible) from the Harbour Station platforms and The Cob is known as Ballast Island (Cei Balast). Two hundred years ago, ships leaving Porthmadog harbour were built to be heavily laden with slate for export to other parts of the world. On their return, these ships inevitably carried less cargo, so to ensure their seaworthiness for the journey back to Porthmadog, their holds were filled with 'ballast' made up of rocks, stone and soil. Once back in Porthmadog the ballast was originally offloaded in an area called 'Rotten Tare' (close to where Porthmadog Maritime Museum stands today). When this became full, ships started to deposit ballast on a sandy bank to the east and this in time grew into Ballast Island. What is remarkable about this island is that it has been created using rocks and soil from every corner of the globe, making it a geological treasure trove. Not only that, some plant seeds contained within the ballast soil survived their voyage across the oceans and germinated on the island, creating a localised flora unlike any other within North Wales.

Top: Ballast Island (Ron Fisher)

Below: Porthmadog Harbour Station

Maritime Museum

Just a couple of minutes' stroll from Harbour Station will bring you to the Maritime Museum, which is situated on the Oakeley Wharf and housed in one of the original slate storage sheds next to the Harbour Master's Office. Here you will find a fascinating collection of artifacts depicting the seafaring activities of the area and the development and history of the port. You will also be able to learn about the world-famous topsail schooners and other vessels built at Porthmadog, the shipwrights, the voyages the ships undertook and the lives of the men and women who sailed on them.

The All Wales Coast Path

The All Wales Coast Path (see page 36) runs straight through Porthmadog and offers delightful and well-signposted walks both to the east and the west. To the east it follows the mile-long (1.6 kms) sea wall known as The Cob (which also carries the Sustrans cycle route 'Lon Las Cymru North' (NCN Route 8/82). From the sea wall there are magnificent views out to sea and inland to the mountains of Snowdonia including one of the best views of Snowdon itself. At the eastern end of The Cob the Path reaches Boston Lodge which is the main engineering works for the Ffestiniog and Welsh Highland Railways and listed in the Guinness Book of Records as being the oldest of its kind in the world. Steam locomotives have been built on this site during the 19th, 20th and 21st centuries. The first, a Double Fairlie engine called Merddin Emrys, was built in 1879 and is still in regular use today. The latest locomotive being built at Boston Lodge is also

a Double Fairlie and will be called James Spooner in honour of the man who surveyed the original route of the Ffestiniog Railway. It is expected to be completed in 2023.

To the south-west the All Wales Coast Path passes through Porthmadog harbour and within 15 minutes you are in the pretty coastal village of Borth y Gest with its array of colourful houses and cafes clustered around a sheltered bay with hidden sandy coves and sea cliffs beyond.

Welsh Highland Heritage Railway

There are in total three railway stations in Porthmadog. At the opposite end of the High Street to the Ffestiniog & Welsh Highland Railways' Harbour Station is Porthmadog Station for the standard-gauge Cambrian Coast Railway which is run by Transport for Wales. This is part of the National Rail network and provides services from Porthmadog to Birmingham in the east, Pwllheli to the west and has connections to Aberystwyth in the south.

Opposite the Cambrian Coast Railway Station is the Welsh Highland Heritage Railway (see page 41). Here you can have a short ride on a heritage narrow-gauge locomotive, visit the engine shed with its fascinating collection of historical railway artifacts, climb aboard a footplate and see for yourself how a locomotive works and even take a ride on a miniature railway. This is a great place to visit if you have young children. www.whr.co.uk

Bringing the Welsh Highland Railway back to life

As we saw at the beginning of this guidebook (pages 4-5 A Brief History of the Welsh Highland Railway) the original Welsh Highland Railway closed to passenger traffic at the end of the summer of 1936 and to all goods traffic the following year. Then in 1941 both the track and rolling stock were requisitioned by the Ministry of Defence for the War Effort.

In the decades following the Second World War, the track bed and railway infrastructure gradually became derelict, other than a short section near Gelert's Farm, Porthmadog, which was restored by the Welsh Highland Railway (1964) Co. Ltd during the 1960s.

In 1989 the Ffestiniog Railway decided to renew its interest in the WHR and made a bid for the original track bed. In 1995, following several years of legal entanglement and a public enquiry (with intervention by the then Secretary of State for Transport John Prescott) the Ffestiniog Railway gained control of the Welsh Highland Railway from the Official Receiver. In the same year the Millennium Commission awarded a

grant of £4.3 million to the Ffestiniog Railway towards the re-construction of the WHR between Caernarfon and Rhyd Ddu.

The plan was to start re-construction at Caernarfon and rebuild backwards to Porthmadog, where the line would connect with the Ffestiniog Railway line to Blaenau Ffestiniog, offering a combined steam railway journey of 40 miles (64kms).

Work started between Caernarfon and Dinas in 1997 and following the clearance of vegetation and repairs to the old track bed, a team of volunteers laid the new track in time for the first train to travel along this section on 13th October 1997. Initially the trains consisted of five new carriages. Subsequently a Pullman car (Bodysgallen) and two more semi-open carriages were added to the fleet. Additional rolling stock was also 'borrowed' from the Ffestiniog Railway, including several locomotives from time to time.

From an early stage it was envisaged that the railway would operate at speeds up to 25mph (40kms) and haul as many as 12 carriages up gradients of up to 1 in 40. This required some powerful locomotives and so a

Above: *1997 April - Track and wagons await use at Dinas*
Above Right: *1997 October - The very first train arrives at Caernarfon*
Below: *1999 September - As far as the line went - Dinas*
Right: *1999 September - Track clearance near Waunfawr*

number of Beyer Garratt (see pages 54-55) locomotives were sourced from South Africa.

The next section of line planned for re-construction was from Dinas to Rhyd Ddu with an estimated rebuilding cost of £9 million. Grants from the European Regional Development Fund, Welsh Development Agency, Welsh Tourist Board and the Welsh Highland Railway Society (amongst others) added to what was left from the original Millennium Commission grant of £4.3 million, enabled work to proceed. The section of railway from Dinas to Waunfawr opened in August 2000 and work started almost immediately on the next section from Waunfawr to Rhyd Ddu, however this was delayed due to restrictions put in place during the Foot and Mouth Disease outbreak in 2001.

Eventually, the section to Rhyd Ddu was completed and officially opened by His Royal Highness the Prince of Wales on 18th August 2003.

Whilst these developments were taking place the Welsh Highland Railway (1964) Co. Ltd (now registered as the Welsh Highland Railway Ltd but known as The Welsh Highland Heritage Railway) reached agreement with the Ffestiniog Railway to rebuild the railway to Pont Croesor and to run trains of heritage rolling stock on this section of line until it was required for completing the route from Caernarfon to Porthmadog

In September 2004 the Ffestiniog Railway received funding of £5 million from the Welsh Assembly and the EU. This, together with funds raised from public appeal, meant that re-construction of the section from Rhyd Ddu to Pont Croesor (via Beddgelert and the Aberglaslyn Pass) and subsequently onwards to Porthmadog, could be undertaken. This was no small task and included volunteers laying 12 miles (19 kms) of track, rebuilding four tunnels and four large river bridges, creating a crossing over the standard gauge Cambrian Coast Line and 'street running' across Britannia Bridge in Porthmadog High Street to connect with the Ffestiniog Railway line in Harbour Station Porthmadog.

Work commenced in 2005 and on 28th February 2009 a 'Golden Bolt' ceremony took place near Harbour Station Porthmadog, when the final bolt was fitted to mark the physical completion of the tracklaying.

Top: *October 2007: laying track in the Aberglaslyn Pass* (John Ellis Williams)

Right: *Golden 2009: A Golden bolt joins together the Ffestiniog and Welsh Highland Railways*

Below: *Her Majesty Queen Elizabeth II naming WHR Pullman Observation Carriage 'Glaslyn'*

On April 27th 2010 Her Majesty Queen Elizabeth II travelled on the Welsh Highland Railway from Caernarfon to Dinas Station where she officially named the WHR's new Observation Pullman Carriage 'Glaslyn'. Finally, on the 30th October 2010 the first passenger trains operated from Caernarfon all the way to Porthmadog carrying, amongst others, those who had supported and sponsored the project.

Top: *April 2007: Volunteer track laying above Beddgerlert* (John Ellis Williams)

Volunteering for the Welsh Highland Railway

It has long been recognised that without the tireless work of its many volunteers, the Welsh Highland Railway would find it almost impossible to operate. The volunteers are an integral part of the WHR and offer support to just about every department, from maintaining the track to looking after passengers.

Featured below are the stories of six WHR volunteers.

David Smith - Guard, Signalman and Controller

"I have always liked railways and have many happy memories of childhood holidays near Aberdaron, during which we would always visit either the Ffestiniog Railway or the ever-growing Welsh Highland Railway. My first volunteering experience was in 2010, when my Explorer Scout group came to the Railway for a week working with the drains gang. We came a few times and then the following year, as part of my Duke of Edinburgh Award, I did a week working as a buffet steward and loved it so much that I came back the following year for a week. That was when I got chatting to a couple of guards, as they looked like they were having fun and that encouraged me to start guard's training in November 2012. I qualified in August 2013 and after that went on to qualify as a signalman in 2015 and a controller in 2016.

I now volunteer in all three disciplines as often as my work schedule allows. I love everything about the Railway, its history, the fact that we are still using locomotives and machinery originally manufactured over 150 years ago and because the view from a guard's van or the signal box is rather better than from my office window in Birmingham!

However, what has really made me stick around has been the people. It's no exaggeration to say that some of my best friends are people I've met working on the Railway, including some that are first-language Welsh and that in turn has spurred me on to learn Welsh, which I've been doing for a few years now. "

Jim Comerford - Black Hand Gang and Tuesday Engineers Group

"I joined the Welsh Highland Railway Society (WHRS) and started volunteering in 1997. At the time I was working in TV broadcasting and to have the opportunity to volunteer outside, even in the Welsh liquid sunshine, was a welcome change to my working life, plus it also gave me a fantastic new set of friends and I gained a new social life too.

At the time work was ongoing to re-build the WHR line and I joined one of the two groups working on the track, the Black Hand Gang as it is known (our hands were always black with grease and oil). Like so many others, I had previously walked through the Glaslyn tunnels, so being involved with the re-build of that section was a fantastic opportunity.

Although the re-build is now complete, I still volunteer with the BHG on a regular basis. There are always a multitude of jobs that need to be done to maintain and improve the infrastructure of the railway, not to mention helping out with events such as the Santa Trains which are organised by the Society.

Once I retired I had a little more time on my hands and I felt that I would like to expand my (very limited) engineering skills, so I also joined the Tuesday Engineers Group, which has been wonderful, as it has not only taught me new skills but has given me hands-on experience with the locomotives too.

Over the past 25 years volunteering on the Railway has given me such a lot. There really is something suitable for everyone, so why not come and give it a go?"

Gary Brindle - Permanent Way

"*I actually live in Porthmadog, so just a stone's throw from the Ffestiniog & Welsh Highland Railway and the terminus for both lines at Harbour Station, so I've had an interest in (and travelled on) the Railway a lot over the years.*

However, I had never taken that first step to getting involved as a volunteer until 2016, when, after a conversation with a couple of existing volunteers, I was invited to join the North Wales Track Gang, which met every other weekend and was part of the Permanent Way section of the Railway. Permanent Way being the route of the railway itself.

I decided to give it a go and since joining I have been given the opportunity to learn many new skills, as well as work with a great bunch of people.

Jobs I've been involved with include laying new railway track and carrying out maintenance on in-service track to ensure a nice smooth ride for those travelling on the trains. I've also carried out maintenance work on the station platforms, including erecting traditional wooden picket style fences around the platforms and I have been involved with cutting back vegetation and trees from the sides of the line to allow clear passage."

Jo Charles - Station and On-Train Host

"*I'm one of the newer volunteers, having only started to help out in June 2021. I live in Bethesda and up until my retirement in 2019 had been working for the NHS here in North Wales for 36 years. So, living locally I've been able to enjoy travelling on the Railway for years, especially when my children were young. I remember often thinking that volunteers on the Railway looked like they were having fun, so once I'd retired and things began to open up again after the Pandemic, I thought I would like to give it a try. What particularly appealed to me was the thought of being part of something local and of such importance to our local economy.*

I've always enjoyed talking to people, so volunteering as a Station Host is just perfect as my role involves welcoming passengers when they first arrive at the station, giving them key information about times of their journey, answering any questions they have and pointing them in the direction of the loos, café and shop before they get on board.

Once on board, the role of the On-Train host is to find out a little bit about the passengers and then add to whatever they may already know, telling them about the journey and sights of interest to look out for along the way.

Being able to travel on the trains through the beautiful scenery is such a privilege, I never get tired of it and I love being part of the wonderful team that works out of Caernarfon. The welcome I had from everyone when I started was lovely and I now have a real sense of being valued."

Ben McCormick -
Trainee Guard & The Black Hand Gang

"I can remember my first visit to the Welsh Highland Railway, I was only four at the time and I have been in love with it ever since. I'm fascinated by engineering and anything technical, so the railway is perfect for me and what is great is that my volunteering enables me to learn new skills all the time. I first volunteered in 2016 and it has become more regular as time has gone on.

In my paid job I'm an office worker, so it is great to spend some of my spare time doing something completely different. With the Black Hand Gang the work can vary from building and track work to making fences and keeping the railway tidy. It's so rewarding to be part of keeping the trains running. Being able to see things you have worked on and accomplished as you travel on the train is really satisfying.

I'm really enjoying training to become a guard; it is great experience and allows me to be involved with running the trains and meeting passengers. I also get involved with some of the events that the Railway holds, such as the SuperPower weekends.

However probably the best job is getting to be an elf at Christmas on the Santa Trains, it's terrific fun!"

Jen Pemberton -
Engineering Department

"I think I was about 12 when I first started volunteering for the Ffestiniog & Welsh Highland Railways. My aunt and uncle had a cottage in Blaenau Ffestiniog and we used to race to see the trains as they came into town. One day in the late 1980s my uncle got talking to Eileen Clayton who looked after the Parks & Gardens Department for the Ffestiniog Railway and soon after that we started volunteering as a family. It was great fun and it taught me many skills including gardening, bricklaying, tiling and painting.

As I grew up I got married and had my own kids and for a while was so busy I didn't get the chance to visit or volunteer for the Railway for one reason or another. Luckily however I still had lots of friends who worked on the Railway and so a few years ago I was able to revisit and begin volunteering again. This time on the Welsh Highland Railway, helping to renovate the NG15 Class Locomotive Number 134.

Getting back on to the Railway, in particular being amongst the engines again has been absolutely brilliant. I didn't realise how much I missed being around the people too.

When I was last up (I live near Solihull) I asked if my dad Bob Anderson would like to join me. He had been an engineer apprentice, so I think he liked the idea of getting his hands dirty again. He said only the other day how great it was that he now has a use for all the tools and equipment he used during his apprenticeship all those years ago.

It's wonderful to think that all these years later we are once again volunteering as a family."

Megan Smith explains how to find out more about Volunteering for the FF & WHR

Megan Smith - Volunteer Fireman and Cymdeithas Rheilffordd Eryri (Welsh Highland Railway Society) Board Director - explains why volunteering for the Welsh Highland Railway is such a great thing to do.

I first began volunteering for the Welsh Highland Railway (WHR) whilst I was studying Sports Coaching & Performance at University in Lancashire. Throughout my childhood, my family and I had spent a lot of time in and around the Snowdonia National Park, specifically Porthmadog and so with long university summer holidays to fill, it seemed like the perfect opportunity to give something back to the Railway I had enjoyed travelling on as a child.

I contacted the Railway via email expressing my interest and before I knew it, I was cleaning engines at Boston Lodge! I took a particular interest in the WHR Garratts, taking great pride in being an engine cleaner and knowing that I was doing my part to help the Railway. My positive attitude and willingness to learn helped me gain the basic skills required to work my way up to the footplate and then on to becoming a trainee fireman on the WHR.

I soon learnt there was a lot more to being a fireman than throwing coal haphazardly onto the fire. Firing is a huge balancing act, a golden triangle of fire, water and pressure. It's important to keep these at an optimal level for the engines to perform as efficiently as possible. This is easier said than done when I am also keeping a look out (for sheep on the line mostly), calling signals, exchanging tokens and keeping myself fuelled with Jaffa cakes! Since qualifying, I have been learning more than ever. No two days are the same. Each day provides me with a different challenge which continues to test my physical abilities and problem-solving skills, as well as my knowledge of the Railway and the local area.

Being on the Board of Director's for Cymdeithas Rheilffordd Eryri (Welsh Highland Railway Society), provides me with a different type of challenge, as my role revolves around the volunteering aspects of the WHR and allows me to give something back to this exceptional Society. My role on the Board brings me full circle. I came to the WHR as a new volunteer and now I have the opportunity to encourage others to come and be part of something very special. I feel proud to be involved in something so rewarding and important.

Our volunteers play a crucial role in maintaining and running the Railway. If you're currently reading this guidebook on one of our trains, sat on a bench on one of our platforms, or in one of our station shops or cafes, the chances are that some of the staff you see around you are volunteers. We simply couldn't function without them.

We are a friendly bunch and when staying over we spend most of our evenings socialising with other volunteers in the Hostels, local restaurants, or pubs. It's great fun, so why not come and join us?

If you would like to be a part of our world class Railway and volunteer on and around the WHR, this is your opportunity.

To begin your journey with us, and become part of the Railway family, simply send an email to our dedicated volunteering email address: **volunteer@ffwhr.com**

We look forward to seeing you soon.

Volunteer Megan Smith

Slate and the
Ffestiniog & Welsh Highland Railways

Over the past two hundred years the Ffestiniog & Welsh Highland Railways, its predecessors and the slate quarries of North Wales have been dominant and intertwined players in the historical, industrial and cultural development of the region.

Today, they are still an integral part of Snowdonia and at least one of the reasons why tens of thousands of people choose to visit the area every year. Be it to sedately travel on beautifully restored heritage steam trains through the UK, or to hurtle across blue lagoons at speeds close to 100mph (161 kms) and through underground caverns attached to little more than a length of metal cable!

However, neither the slate industry or the railways could have offered such present-day diverse experiences, or indeed been anything like as successful, without the other.

Without the railways, the production of slate and in particular its transportation from the quarries located high in the mountains to ships waiting at berth in the harbours of Porthmadog and Caernarfon, was a slow, arduous and ultimately unprofitable affair.

Likewise, there would have been no reason to build the railways in the first place if not to service the developing slate industry. Prior to the 19th century the population of North Wales and Snowdonia in particular, had little use for railways. They lived in remote, sparse settlements, surviving predominantly on farming and what could be scratched from the land.

So, what was it that turned the quarrying of slate (which had existed, albeit on a small scale, since the Roman period, when slate was used to roof the Roman fort at Segontium near Caernarfon) into one of the most important industries of the Victorian era?

Well, up to the end of the 18th century, slate was extracted by independent groups of quarrymen who paid a royalty to the landowner and used horses and carts to transport the slate to port or market.

However, by the beginning of the 19th century the industrial revolution was building up steam, factories were springing up throughout Britain, agricultural workers were leaving the fields to work in the factories and those workers needed housing and those houses (along with the factories themselves) needed roofs – slate roofs.

Above: *Zip World, Llechwedd quarry, Blaenau Ffestiniog*
Left: *In 1893 nearly 20,000 men worked in the North Wales slate industry*
Below: *Houses sprung up around the factories and they all needed slate roofs.*

Left: *Re-enactment of an Victorian gravity train.* (Chris Clark)

Below: *Slate quays at Porthmadog Harbour*

Suddenly slate was in demand everywhere, not just in Britain, but across the Empire. It didn't take long for the landowners, who had previously simply leased out their land to the quarrymen, to realise there was more money to be made by operating the quarries themselves. Nor did it take them long to lobby the British Government, who up to this point had charged a 20% slate duty on every ton of slate extracted, asking them to abolish this tax.

In August 1831 the Government abolished the duty and the North Wales slate industry went into rapid expansion, with over 20 new quarries opening in the next ten years. In 1793 slate production was 26,000 tons, a century later it was over half a million tons and the industry employed close on 20,000 men, plus thousands more employed in ancillary services.

To aid this expansion the quarry owners knew they needed to improve their transportation links, horse and cart had had its day, now it was the turn of the railway. Railways sprung up throughout the region, servicing the main quarries around Llanberis, Bethesda and Blaenau Ffestiniog, with many smaller tramways linking into these lines along their route to the ports.

The Ffestiniog Railway was constructed between 1833 and 1836 deliberately to link the slate quarries around Blaenau Ffestiniog with the harbour at Porthmadog.

However, the Welsh Highland Railway line you are following today did not come into operation until 1881 and even then, it was only part of the present-day route.

In 1872 Charles Spooner of the Ffestiniog Railway proposed a new narrow-gauge line linking the standard gauge London and North Western Railway at Dinas Junction near Caernarfon with Rhyd Ddu at the foot of Snowdon. It was built between 1877 and 1881 and was originally called the North Wales Narrow Gauge Railways. This line transported both dressed slate and passengers nine and a half miles (15kms) from the Glanrafon Slate Quarry (see page 17) near Rhyd Ddu to Dinas Junction (see page 22). Spooner also instigated the construction of a three-mile (4.8kms) narrow-gauge branch-line from Dinas to the quarries above Bryngwyn (see page 23).

In 1923 the Dinas to Rhyd Ddu line was extended south from Rhyd Ddu to link up with the Croesor Tramway (see page 9), which had been built in 1864 to connect slate quarries in the Croesor valley with Porthmadog.

The completed line, now called for the first time the Welsh Highland Railway, came into service on 1st June 1923. However, with the decline in the production of slate the line closed in 1937, whereupon it fell into disrepair until the 1990s when work begun in earnest to restore and reopen the route from Caernarfon to Porthmadog.

To find out more about the restoration of the Welsh Highland Railway see pages 40-41.

Slate Landscape of Northwest Wales Awarded Unesco World Heritage Status

In July 2021 it was announced that the slate landscape of North Wales had been awarded UNESCO World Heritage Status. This remarkable achievement ranks the importance of the Snowdonia slate industry and its transportation links alongside other iconic landscapes such as the Grand Canyon in the USA, Machu Picchu in Peru, the Great Pyramids in Egypt and the Taj Mahal in India.

In making the award UNESCO said...................

The Slate Landscape of Northwest Wales represents an exceptional example of an industrial cultural landscape that was profoundly shaped by large-scale slate quarrying and underground mining and by the working and transport of slate for national and international markets.

This new World Heritage Site comprises six distinct areas including spectacular quarry landscapes such as Penrhyn, Dinorwig, the Nantlle Valley and Ffestiniog. It also includes the National Slate Museum in Llanberis, Penrhyn Castle near Bangor and the Ffestiniog Railway, built specifically to transport slate from quarry to port and later transformed, predominantly through the dedication of volunteers, into a working heritage railway and latterly into one of the major tourist attractions of the region.

Above: *Penrhyn Castle* (Tony Russell)

Below: *The Welsh Highland Railway line runs directly below Glanrafon Slate Quarry near Rhyd Ddu*

This UNESCO World Heritage status shows recognition of the significant contribution North Wales and in particular the county of Gwynedd, has made to the cultural and industrial heritage not only of Wales, but of the wider world. Welsh slate can be found on roofs all over the world including the Houses of Parliament, 10 Downing Street, Buckingham Palace, Melbourne's Royal Exhibition Building in Australia and Copenhagen City Hall in Denmark. In the Victorian era over half the buildings of New York had roofs of Welsh slate.

Quarrying and mining of slate in Gwynedd has left a unique legacy which local communities are rightly proud of and it is one of the reasons given for the survival of the Welsh language. Slate quarrying has been described as 'the most Welsh of Welsh industries', being the only major industry in the British Isles that throughout its history has been conducted in a language other than English.

So, going forward, what does this mean for the region? Well, the whole point of World Heritage Status is that it offers worldwide recognition and understanding of the importance of a landscape, its legacy, heritage and its cultural significance. This in turn will help protect, conserve and preserve that legacy and its history for generations to come as well as helping with future regeneration.

One benefit sited for this award, is that it will help deflect some of the effects of mass tourism which 'honeypot sites' such as Yr Wyddfa (Snowdon) have experienced in recent years. The UNESCO status will help people understand and appreciate that the region is more than just one mountain and encourage visitors to explore and find out more about the slate industry, its landscapes and the culture surrounding it. It is hoped that this in turn will bring economic benefits to areas that up to now have not benefitted from tourism.

One new initiative already in operation is the Snowdonia Slate Trail, Llwybr Llechi Eryri, which is an 83-mile (133-km) circular trail which enables walkers to explore the industrial heritage of the North Wales slate industry and its associated villages throughout Snowdonia. **https://snowdoniaslatetrail.org/**

The route starts at Porth Penrhyn near Bangor and ends at Bethesda in the Nant Ffrancon valley. In between it passes through Llanberis, Waunfawr, Nantlle, Beddgelert, Tanygrisiau, Blaenau Ffestiniog, Betws y Coed and Capel Curig.

The UNESCO award has also helped attract over £1million of external investment in projects which will interpret the slate industries' heritage and culture. Art projects in primary and secondary schools and plans for colourful and striking murals in many slate towns and villages are already being developed.

New projects will also look at regenerating areas through culture and heritage, creating new business and employment opportunities, improving provision and co-ordinated experiences across the area, improving sustainable transport and developing more interpretation and education of the slate industry and the Welsh language.

One such project already underway is the Ffestiniog Railway's Boston Lodge Redevelopment and Interpretation Project (to find out more see pages 50 – 51).

Top: *Announcement of UNESCO World Heritage status at the National Slate Museum in Llanberis*

Below: *Remnants of the slate industry can be found all over North Wales*

Boston Lodge
Redevelopment & Interpretation Project

In October 2021, the Ffestiniog & Welsh Highland Railways secured a £3.1 million National Lottery Heritage Fund (NLHF) grant towards a £4.2 million project to restore, redevelop and interpret the Railways' historic workshops at Boston Lodge, Porthmadog.

Boston Lodge Works is in the Guinness Book of Records as 'the oldest railway engineering workshop in continuous operation in the world'. It was opened in 1842 to provide engineering support for the Ffestiniog Railway, which was itself built between 1833 and 1836 to transport slate from the quarries around Ffestiniog to the port at Porthmadog, from where it was shipped across the world.

Prior to this period the Boston Lodge site had been the main quarry, workshops and barracks for those constructing the adjacent sea wall, land reclamation embankment known as The Cob between 1808 and 1811. It was these earlier workshops (known as the Top Yard) which were expanded to support the operation of the Ffestiniog Railway in its early horse-drawn form from the 1830s to the 1860s.

The current Project has two primary aims. The first is to improve interpretation of the historical significance of the Ffestiniog & Welsh Highland Railways, its

workshops, its connection with the landscape in which it sits and its importance to the slate industry that has had such a profound effect on the area. The second aim is to secure the future of the historic railway works site at Boston Lodge by conserving the remaining 19th century buildings, which include the original blacksmith's premises and barracks, so that they can continue to function effectively in the 21st century and beyond, as well as improving access and constructing a new small locomotive shed.

More than 250,000 people a year visit the Ffestiniog & Welsh Highland Railways, which became part of the

UNESCO Slate Heritage of North West Wales World Heritage Site in July 2021 (see pages 48-49). However, as the generations move on there is a concern that the major national (and international) historical significance of the Railway and of the slate industry that it was built to serve, will become less apparent to those visitors. The Project will address this through a comprehensive and ambitious interpretation plan which will ultimately allow visitors to tour the site, including the original Engineering Shed (see photograph below) and experience its unique history first-hand.

Guided tours will be central to this plan and in time the Railway will be seeking volunteers who would like to help deliver site interpretation and guided tours at Boston Lodge. To find out more about volunteering for the Ffestiniog & Welsh Highland Railways see pages 42-45 of this guidebook.

The project, which is to be staged over five years, will also provide for the local community, new jobs, training and volunteering opportunities in engineering, maintenance and building work.

Top: *Boston Lodge 1887*
Below: *Boston Lodge old engine shed 1887*

Plas Brondanw Gardens

Plas Brondanw is the 16th century ancestral home of Portmeirion architect Sir Clough Williams Ellis. It is located near the villages of Garreg and Llanfrothen and five minutes' drive from Pont Croesor Station on the Welsh Highland Railway. Surrounding Plas Brondanw are beautiful gardens laid out in Arts & Crafts style by Sir Clough during the first two decades of the 20th century.

Sir Clough was given Plas Brondanw (in a rather dilapidated state) by his father in 1904 and immediately began to restore the house and create a landscaped garden around it.

Clough & Amabel Williams-Ellis, 1975 (Clough Williams-Ellis Foundation)

Inspired by the Arts and Crafts movement, the garden at Plas Brondanw is reminiscent of Hidcote with its intimate garden 'rooms', enclosed by dense close-clipped yew hedging. However, this is not a garden which forces you to look inwards, far from it. Sir Clough understood the surrounding majestic Snowdonia landscape must be embraced, so throughout the garden you are constantly reminded of what lies beyond. Hazy-blue ridgelines are glimpsed through archways and dramatic reveals appear at the end of pathways, such as the one perfectly aligned on the Matterhorn-like peak of Cnicht. Today, it is also possible to see the steam trains of the Welsh Highland Railway making their way through this beautiful landscape.

www.plasbrondanw.com/gardens

Top: *Plas Brondanw Gardens* (Tony Russell)

Above: *Avenue aligned on Cnicht* (Tony Russell)

Below: *Plas Brondanw dates from the 16th century* (Tony Russell)

Glaslyn Osprey Centre

The Osprey Visitor Centre of Bywyd Gwyllt Glaslyn Wildlife (a registered charity) is located adjacent to Pont Croesor Station on the Welsh Highland Railway. From here it is possible to view some of the first Ospreys to breed in Wales for more than a century. This can be done using binoculars, telescopes (provided) and live screens linked to webcams positioned less than two metres from the nest. Well-informed volunteers are on hand to answer all questions and provide visitors with the latest information.

Ospreys first returned to the Glaslyn Valley in 2004, choosing to nest in a Silver Fir tree near to the line of the Welsh Highland Railway. With close proximity to both the Glaslyn River and the sea beyond The Cob at Porthmadog, it is the prefect location for these magnificent fish-eating birds.

Remarkably the same female Osprey that first nested in the Glaslyn Valley in 2004 has returned to the same nesting site every year since and todate (spring 2022) has successfully fledged 41 chicks! Affectionally known as 'Glaslyn Lady' or 'Mrs G', she is one of the most prolific breeding Ospreys in the United Kingdom and is now with her second breeding partner called Aran.

www.glaslynwildlife.co.uk

Top: *View towards the osprey nest and Snowdon (Yr Wyddfa)* (Tony Russell)

Above: *Visitor centre for Bywyd Gwyllt Glaslyn Wildlife* (Charles Flint)

Below: *Young Glaslyn ospreys from 2014*

Beyer Garratt locomotives on the Welsh Highland Railway

If you are travelling on the Welsh Highland Railway then it is quite likely that your train is being hauled by one of our Beyer Garratt locomotives. These locomotives are articulated, which allows them to negotiate tight curves in the track that would be impossible for rigid-frame locomotives to achieve. There are several such curves on the route of the Welsh Highland Railway, in particular between Beddgelert and Rhyd Ddu Stations where two large 'S' bends follow the land contours thereby allowing the trains to gain height (or lose height depending on the direction of travel) on one of the steepest railway gradients in Britain, nominally 1 in 40.

Each Beyer Garratt locomotive is comprised of three main parts. A front engine and water tank with its own set of wheels and cylinders. A rear engine and coal bunker also with one set of wheels and cylinders. Suspended between the two is a large boiler, firebox and driving cab, which pivots on each of the two engines and thereby provides the articulation necessary to negotiate the curves. Another benefit of Beyer Garratt locomotives is the fact that having two engines effectively doubles the power of conventional locomotives. This is very important on the Welsh Highland Railway as these locomotives have to be strong enough to haul up to ten carriages full of passengers through the undulating landscapes of Snowdonia.

The Beyer Garratt articulated locomotive was the brainchild of English mechanical engineer Herbert William Garratt (1864 – 1913). They were designed and built to Garratt's newly granted patent at the Gorton Foundry of Beyer Peacock in Manchester between 1909 and 1958. Initially they were to 1ft 11 ½ inches (597mm) narrow gauge specification (as in use today on the Welsh Highland Railway) but standard gauge Garratt locomotives soon followed. In all over 1,000 Beyer Garratt articulated locomotives were built.

Left: *NGG16 No.87 sits outside Boston Lodge Works*

Centre Left & Right: *Extra tanks are useful for longer journeys.*

Bottom Right: *Garratt K1's primitive design and smaller tanks make it less useful on today's longer services.*

The first two Garratt locomotives ever built (in 1909) were known as 'K' Class (K1 and K2) and were built for service on the North East Dundas Tramway in Tasmania. In 1947 K1 returned to Britain to become a museum piece at Beyer Peacock's Gorton Foundry. When the foundry closed in the 1960s the locomotive was purchased by the Ffestiniog Railway where it was partially restored and displayed at Harbour Station in Porthmadog before being placed on loan to the National Railway Museum in York. K1 returned to Wales in 2000 and eventually, after further restoration work, made its maiden journey on the Welsh Highland Railway in September 2006, where it remained in service until 2014 when its boiler certificate expired.

The final Garratts built to a Beyer Peacock design eight 1ft 11 ½ inches (597mm) narrow gauge Class NGG16 locomotives, all built for South African Railways. Of these the very last one to be built (and indeed the last steam locomotive ever to be built by Beyer Peacock at the Gorton Foundry Manchester) was NGG16 No.143 which was built in 1958. This, along with four other Garratt locomotives, are now in the care of the Ffestiniog & Welsh Highland Railways.

In December 2019 K1 was moved to Statfold Barn Railway near Tamworth, initially for display but then for work that would allow the locomotive to re-enter service. It was back in steam in March 2020 and eventually returned to the Welsh Highland Railway in September 2021.

During 2022 NGG16 No's 87 and 130 (the rebuild completed in Spring of 2021) should be in regular operation with No's 138 and 143 being overhauled and 140 awaiting a rebuild.

At Your Service -
Welsh Highland Railway 2022 style!

If you have not ordered a hamper in advance, food may be purchased at Caernarfon and Porthmadog Stations and taken on board. Light refreshments to take away are also available from our friendly team at Beddgelert Station.

Far Left: *The elegance of the Pullman obsevation carriage set up for tea. Carefully designed perspex dividers go almost unseen*

Far Left Lower: *Hampers ready to go!*

Left & Below: *The mezzanine floor in Caffi de Winton has splendid views of the Castle and Cei Llechi and may be hired for private parties.*

Caffi De Winton

At Caernarfon Station, our modern style Caffi De Winton overlooking the harbour and adjacent castle is popular with visitors and locals alike serving freshly cooked light meals and some very tasty cakes. They have a passion for sourcing local produce such as their meat from widely renowned butchers Owen Glyn Owen & Son in Caernarfon and award winning Snowdonia Cheese. You might fancy a bottle of beer from local craft brewery Bragdy Lleu to accompany your lunch. The mezzanine floor is popular with small groups and may be booked for a private party. For more information, telephone 01286 677018 or find 'Y Stesion' on Facebook.

Our staff are local and proud of their new station and always happy to help with your culinary needs.

Our customer service and care are at the forefront of everything we do and over the past two years this has added to passenger confidence and been really appreciated by all our visitors.

We hope that if you are travelling with us, you have booked your experience online and been sent an email with useful information such as where to park and what time to arrive. We think that knowing your space is booked and waiting for you on the train makes life less stressful. We have decided to retain the Perspex dividers for the time being. We think they look quite smart and give your group just a little more privacy.

When not able to provide a buffet car refreshment service, we came up with the alternative of a picnic hamper and these have proved such a hit that we are continuing with them! Tasty rolls made up in our own cafes and who could resist a Pullman Pamper Hamper as you enjoy your first class 'Gold' experience? Simply book these along with your tickets.

Top Left: *Train spotting at its best - Spooner's beer terrace*

Below: *Spooner's bar area*

Bottom Left: *Gifts from the shop*

Bottom Right: *A warm welcome from some of our volunteer hosts*

Spooner's at Porthmadog

Spooner's Café and Bar at Porthmadog Harbour Station is a large multi-functional space in the station's old Goods Shed. By day it is a busy café serving passengers with a range of hot and cold snacks and meals. The beer terrace on the platform is hugely popular, especially on a sunny day and what better place to watch the trains go by as well as enjoy the views along The Cob and out to sea! In the evening, Spooner's takes on a pub atmosphere with its wide range of ales and cocktails and bar menu. The walls of Spooner's are adorned with historic photos and railway artefacts making each visit an interesting one.
A small 'coffee to go' takeaway facility can also be found on the platform for those wanting a quick drink or ice cream.

Our Hosts

Right at the front of our customer service team and probably the first people you meet as you arrive at the station to check in, are our station hosts. This great bunch of volunteers have come together over the past couple of years to make sure you are welcomed, feel safe and enjoy your visit. They will help you find your seat, direct you to the nearest café, answer questions on the local area and generally make you feel at home. They are the epitome of what volunteering on the railways is all about. We love them and we are sure you will too. To find out more about our volunteers see pages 42-45 of this guidebook.

Shopping

Both Caernarfon and Porthmadog Stations house extensive gift shops where you can pick up a memento of your day. Both have a good stock of both new and pre-owned books and Porthmadog has a narrow gauge railway modelling section too. There is also an excellent web shop – **www.festshop.co.uk**

How Green is Our Railway?

As custodians of two of the oldest and most scenic narrow-gauge steam railways in Britain, we have three main responsibilities; to protect and conserve the railway and its historic locomotives, to provide an authentic and enjoyable experience for those who travel upon it and to operate a major tourist attraction that is as environmentally friendly as possible.

There is of course no getting away from the fact that we burn coal and to put it simply, without coal there would be no steam locomotives and therefore no authentic heritage railway. However, if you look a little closer you will see we already have a whole raft of systems and procedures in place that ensure our production of carbon is minimal and that the Railway sits comfortably within the beautiful landscapes of the Snowdonia National Park.

Detailed below are just some of the things we are already doing to ensure our Railway(s) are as green and environmentally friendly as possible, as well as information on some of the new and exciting initiatives that we are currently working on;

● Each of our trains transports on average 136 people into the Snowdonia National Park to admire the beautiful scenery. This is the equivalent of taking 45 cars off the road for the duration of their journey with us.

● Our main engineering works at Boston Lodge, where our trains are maintained, restored and even rebuilt, is now powered entirely from solar energy. Banks of solar panels have been installed on the roof of our main carriage shed and these produce up to 80 kilowatts of energy during working hours.

● As well as powering our main Boston Lodge workshops, these same solar panels also store enough energy to enable us to recharge the carriage batteries overnight. Which means when you are travelling on one of our trains, all the energy required for lights, fridges, toilets and anything else that requires onboard electricity has been generated from solar power.

Above Right: *Solar panels on the roof of the Boston Lodge main carriage shed.* **Below:** *New railway sleepers made from recycled plastic*

- All new sleepers used on our railway tracks are made in the UK from recycled plastic. In the past, the Railway would have used hardwood timber from felled trees that had taken anywhere between 60-100 years to reach maturity. The recycled plastic we use would otherwise have either gone into landfill, or been shipped off to Asia, where it may even have ended up in the sea.

- We are currently planning a new station for Beddgelert and it will be as environmentally friendly as possible. We will be using timber from sustainable sources, local building materials and the very latest insulation techniques. The whole building will be powered by solar energy and will also include a rainwater capture system. In addition to this, Beddgelert is one of the stations where our locomotives take on water, so we are looking to harvest rainwater for this purpose too.

- Looking a little further into the future, we are planning for all our diesel locomotives and engines that currently service the Railway, for example working on shunting duties, on emergency work, maintaining the track and the lineside etc., to be converted from diesel to battery powered, with the batteries being charged from solar energy. This will help reduce our consumption of fossil fuels, whilst at the same time ensuring that the trains our passengers travel on will still offer the same authentic travel experience that has existed since the Victorian era.

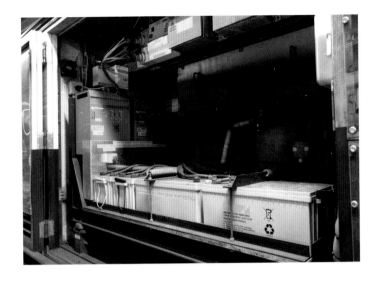

Top: *Storing solar energy to recharge our carriages*
Above: *Our solar panels at Boston Lodge produce up to 80 kilowatts of energy*
Below: *Planning for our locomotives to use harvested rainwater*